# SO YOU THOUGHT YOU KNEW

"A fresh wind is sweeping 21st century Christianity. It challenges our assumptions, it invigorates our faith and it motivates us to love. Joshua Tongol is one of those moved by this fresh wind. This book is easy to read yet it is a thought provoking story of a journey with Jesus in his upside-down kingdom. This is one of those rare books where faith and questions both meet in one person's quest for honesty in Christianity. I am reminded of *The Shack*."

**—MICHAEL HARDIN**
**Executive Director of *Preaching Peace***
**and Author of *The Jesus Driven Life***

"In this artful, thoughtful and accessible work, Joshua Tongol asks some very disconcerting questions and offers equally liberating proposals. His challenges should not be misread as simply setting up polarizing binaries. Rather, I believe he's faithfully shaping a generation of critically thinking believers with the capacity to perform a very specific and unlikely miracle: making Christianity possible for my grandchildren. What matters to God and what matters to me is a theology and practice that magnifies the love of God and ministers the love of Christ. The rest, apparently, really is up for grabs."

**—DR. BRAD JERSAK**
**Author of *Can You Hear Me?***
**and *Kissing the Leper***

"Accessible, winsome and provocative, Joshua Tongol has written a powerful book arising out of his own spiritual journey that seeks to inspire 'those who have ears to hear' to step out of their carefully circumscribed faith and into something that more closely resembles the freedom available through Christ."

**—KEVIN MILLER**
**Director of *Hellbound?***

"This brilliantly thought-out, carefully worded and daringly provocative book is a must read for all who ask questions, answer questions and perhaps more importantly, question the answers we've habitually used and traded down for millennia. This book forces us to reconsider what we believe, why we believe it, and whether those beliefs add to or subtract from the quality of our lives."

**—BISHOP CARLTON PEARSON**
**Author of *The Gospel of Inclusion***
**and *God is Not a Christian, Nor a***
***Jew, Muslim, Hindu...***

"In a personable and approachable style, Joshua Tongol fearlessly helps us to face the hard questions of faith so many of us struggle with. This is not a book with "all the answers" so much as it is one that models that it's okay for us to ask those questions as a healthy expression of faith. That can be scary—even isolating—but Joshua continually brings the focus back to a grace that just won't let go, allowing us to have the courage to ask those difficult questions together."

**—DEREK FLOOD**
**Author of *Healing the Gospel: A Radical***
***Vision for Grace, Justice, and the Cross***

"Many of us have inherited a version of the 'good news' that, honestly, doesn't seem very good. We wrestle with the disparity between the god we are told exists, and the God our hearts tell us must exist. Unfortunately, few of us have a conversation partner with which we can process this incongruity. Enter Joshua Tongol. This is more than a book; it's an invitation. An invitation to allow yourself to ask the hard questions of the faith you have inherited. So, grab a beverage, pull up a chair, and allow Josh to give voice to the questions your heart has been asking. I think you might just find something that you can finally call 'good news'."

**—RABORN JOHNSON**
**Co-host of *BeyondtheBoxPodcast*.com**


"Joshua Tongol has restored to Christendom the Good News of God's driving passion to be in a love relationship with all humanity. Beautiful, simple, yet profoundly deep, Joshua calls the church to an authentic Christian way of life that, if lived out, will transform the world. A must-read that will thoroughly, theologically, rock the status quo!"

**—SHARON BAKER**
**Author of *Razing Hell: Rethinking Everything You've Been Taught About God's Wrath and Judgment***

# SO YOU THOUGHT YOU KNEW

*LETTING GO OF RELIGION*

Joshua Tongol

First Printing, 2014
ISBN 978-0-9914639-0-9 (Paperback)

Book Design by Brother Teresa
cargocollective.com/brotherteresa

Joshua Tongol
joshuatongol.com

*For Remy*

# CONTENTS

PREFACE

# A NEW LANGUAGE, A NEW WORLD

*"Speak a new language so that the world will be a new world."*

**—RUMI**

*"We thought that we had the answers It was the questions we had wrong"*

**—BONO**

There is a certain conversation happening all over the world today.

It's a conversation, which has been around for quite some time,[1] but the voices are getting louder and louder even as I write.

It's a conversation making some people feel uncomfortable, while, at the same time, making others upset.

But there's another reaction to this conversation as well—one that is continually growing in number. It's a reaction where people are feeling a sense of freedom for the first time in years.

What is this conversation about? Surprisingly, it's about *rethinking* the Christian faith.

Believe it or not, more and more people—especially these days—are accusing the Christian God (along with his followers) of being
hateful,
exclusive,
judgmental,
and violent.[2]

Whether or not these accusations are true, these have been the thoughts and experiences of many people around the world.

That said, I want to ask you a very important (and maybe uncomfortable) question.

What if *almost* everything you were taught about Christianity is wrong?

I know, I know, it's a scary question for some of us to even think about.

But, what if?

Would you give up on faith altogether? Or is it possible to rediscover—with fresh eyes—a richer and more satisfying understanding of God and spirituality?

I believe a better spirit of Christianity can exist—one which has been forgotten in history and in certain parts of the world, but is, thankfully, being rediscovered by genuine seekers of truth.

It's a Christianity which is ...
more *loving* than hateful,
more *inclusive* than exclusive,
more *tolerant* than judgmental,
and more *peaceful* than violent.

"Is that even possible?" critics might be wondering. Well, that's what *this* book is all about.

You see, I'm no stranger to fundamentalist Christianity.

In fact, I was born into it.

I was a part of the Pentecostal tradition until my late teens. By the age of seventeen, I became more conservative theologically when it came to the miraculous gifts of the Holy Spirit and ended up leaving the Pentecostal church I grew up in.

From then on, I had an obsession with apologetics and my desire was to eventually travel the world and defend the "Christian faith" against all the "false religions and world-views." In my early twenties, I started studying under some well-known theologians, philosophers, and apologists at a popular evangelical school in California.

During those years, I first served as an apologetics teacher at a Presbyterian church, next as a pastor at a Southern Baptist church. Unexpectedly, I experienced a radical shift concerning the miraculous gifts of the Spirit and ended up leaving the Southern Baptist church.

Not long after, I served as an evangelist at an Assemblies of God church. From my mid-to-late twenties I was heavily involved in the charismatic movement and was busy traveling and speaking around the U.S. and abroad.

After graduating from seminary, I became a missionary to the Philippines (which is predominately Roman Catholic). After my first year, I met the love of my life (who happened to have grown up in an Islamic country) and we ended up doing ministry together for several years before moving to America.

Now, I've always been the type to ask questions, but during those years in the Philippines I finally found the courage to *really* ask questions. I'm talking about sincerely questioning some of my *fundamental* beliefs as an evangelical Christian. Come to think of it, even though I studied many of the criticisms against Christianity in times past, and even though some of them actually made sense to me, I still couldn't let go of some of my *core* beliefs as an evangelical. I just couldn't. I was too scared.

So what did I always end up doing?
I read more Christian material to affirm what I *already* believed.

But with all the nagging thoughts, genuine questions, and eye-opening experiences I was having, I just knew—in order to be true to myself—it was time for me to finally let some of my "beliefs" go.

• • •

Throughout this book I'll be sharing some of the major elements of Christianity which have shaped the way I perceived many things as a believer—things such as God, the Bible, the world, the afterlife, evil, etc.—and how rethinking each one of them has expanded my view of love and has changed my view of ... well ... everything.

As you read, you'll watch me bleed and expose my heart as I say it out loud—all of it. You'll see my struggles with religion, my frustrations with life, and my discoveries of truth. I'll boldly say in public what many honest people are thinking in private.

No holding back. No pulling punches.
No sugar-coating. Just straight-up raw.

Like many who have grown up in organized religion, I know what it's like to live in fear of God (the scaredy-cat kind and not the reverent one). I know what it's like to be immersed in legalism. I know what it's like to experience burnout in ministry. And I also know what it's like to have doubts.

This book is an attempt to think outside the "institutional walls" of organized religion and ask the hard questions—the questions many Christians are too afraid to ask without feeling guilty.

You see, I don't think God is afraid of people asking questions. In fact, contrary to those who believe it's a "sin" to do so, I believe God actually welcomes them.

Newsflash: God isn't insecure.

Don't get me wrong, although I'll be sharing some of my honest thoughts on important topics, this book isn't the final word. I'm simply here to add to the conversation. I don't claim to have all the answers. But I am here to question some of the "answers" many of us been given because some of us were sold on a religion which didn't work.

It's about time more of us question the assumptions we've proudly held (uncritically) for too long.

We were told ...
what to believe,
how to think,
and how to live.

Why?
Because that's just what religion did to many of us.

There's a word for this—it's called *indoctrination.*

And that, my friend, is what usually happens when we don't question.

It's about time more of us recognize that the older way of thinking about God seems to be outdated and irrelevant in an ever-changing world. And it's about time we finally become honest with ourselves as seekers who are not willing to stay fixed with traditional beliefs simply for the sake of just that ... tradition.

Because once we stop lying to ourselves and others about what we supposedly "believe," that's when true seeking begins. It becomes a path of total honesty where one says, "I'm going to follow truth wherever it leads me ... no matter what the cost."

• • •

This book is primarily written for the millions of Christians out there who are dissatisfied with legalistic Christianity.

But it's also for those who are ...
hungering for truth,
tired or hurt by religion,
asking honest questions,
tired of pretending to believe,
wanting to hear "real talk" without all the *B.S.*,
and for those who have had moments of doubt at one time or another and have thought, "There must be a better way."

Well, whoever you are, you're not alone.
I'm right there with you.

I want to help readers draw out their deepest convictions, whether they agree with me or not. I want people to think for themselves, to come to their own conclusions, and to be true to what they really believe.

Because what I've seen, at least for the most part, is a *disconnect* between the head and the heart among many religious people.

For instance, they say "amen!" during a sermon being preached because everyone else does, even though they don't mean it. Or they share a particular version of the gospel, one which condemns the majority of humanity to eternal hellfire while hearing a voice within asking, "Do you really believe what you're saying?"

There is a tension,
an uneasiness,
a conflict.

So can both the head *and* the heart come together in agreement?
I think they can.

That being said, I believe much of the content I affirm in these pages is simply a reminder—an awakening—of what you already know.

It's to open your eyes to what you've always believed ... deep down ... in the recesses of your soul ... before religion stole your innocence and wonder.

There is a better message than the "turn or burn" gospel for the world to hear. Because if there is such a thing as the gospel, then I believe it must be good news for the *whole world*, and not only a *select few*.

It's a gospel which will ...
melt away fear,
restore hope,
and inspire to freely live in love.

• • •

Sure, some might be offended with the fact that I'm encouraging Christians to rethink some of their long-held beliefs. Some might even accuse me of stepping out of, according to their estimation, the box of "orthodoxy." And some might even say I've "crossed the line."

Who created the box anyway?
And who is to say where the line should be drawn?

What if the box is supposed to be *bigger*?
And what if the line is in the *wrong place*?

Seriously. What if?

Because whether we like it or not, the world is changing. Some think for the better, while others, however, think for the worst.

Is there a positive paradigm shift happening in Christianity today?

Only time will tell.

Although fear-based religion resists progress and change, I for one, desire it.

*Joshua Tongol*
California, 2014

ONE

# GOD:
# I NO LONGER BELIEVE

*"A god who let us prove his existence would be an idol."*
**—DIETRICH BONHOEFFER**

*"I laugh when I hear that the fish in the water is thirsty."*
**—KABIR**

I have a confession to make:

*I no longer believe God is out there.*

I know that might sound strange coming from a guy like me writing a book like this. But seriously, I really don't. Call me a skeptic of a "certain kind" if you will. Am I an atheist? No, I wouldn't go that far.

I just no longer believe God is out there.

Time and time again, I've attended religious meetings where people would lift their hands up to try and reach out to God.

I've also watched award ceremonies on television where the winners would hold their awards high for all to see—pointing their index finger up in the air—giving thanks to God.

I've seen football players who, after scoring a touchdown, get down on one knee, do the sign of the cross, and look up to the God in the sky in gratitude.

But, like I said, I no longer believe God is out there.

For years I participated in emotionally intense religious meetings where we would cry out to the "God in heaven"—literally at the top of our lungs—asking him to "come down" and "pour out his Spirit."

I've had Christians tell me amazing stories of when they attended boring church services and, out of nowhere, God "showed up" and performed mighty miracles in their midst.

Hearing those types of stories always made me wonder, "Where was God before he 'showed up'?"

I've even attended services where someone would invite the "Holy Spirit to come" towards the end of the meeting—right after the preacher shared his or her message.

But that would get me thinking, "Where was the Holy Spirit at the beginning of the meeting?"

Or how could I forget those lonely nights when I'd sit outside my house, look up at the stars, and ask God, "Where are you?"

Now I'm in my thirties. I have two degrees in theology. I have over ten years of ministry experience. And I've come to this conclusion:

*I no longer believe God is out there.*

• • •

You see, for most of my life I believed God was "out there." Being a Christian, I was even told I could

have a personal relationship with this God.
*Me? And God? Have a relationship? Wow!*

Now that's a pretty big deal, don't you think? Because *relationship* implies a two-way street, doesn't it? You know, I talk to God, and he ... well ... he's supposed to talk back to me, right?

Ironically, and to be completely honest, my relationship with God growing up—at least for the most part—felt more like a *monologue*.

I would talk to God and then ...
*cricket, cricket, cricket.*

Dead silence.

No voice from heaven. No burning bush. No talking jackass. Just me feeling like an ass while waiting several hours for a response from my invisible friend.

I thought, "If God is a true friend,
then why doesn't he talk back?"

Christians had an interesting way of explaining this conundrum to me.

"God," they said, "doesn't necessarily speak through an audible voice, Josh. He speaks through people, circumstances, and the Bible."

OK, but the thing is, I've actually met many Christians, especially within the charismatic tradition,[1] who did seem to have actual back-and-forth conversations with God. So what's up with that?

Was I jealous of them? Heck yes! Many times, actually. Sometimes I wondered if I wasn't special enough for God to speak to me the way he did with others.

. . .

For most of my life, and in spite of my frustrations with my invisible "best friend," I never had major doubts about God's existence. I kept believing God was out there ... still listening to me ... still hearing my prayers ... and still answering them in ways that weren't always so clear to me.

You see, it was God's apparent silence which seemed to bother me the most, especially during the difficult times in my life. Even though I felt alone, I still boasted to others of how I had this unique relationship with God—that he was my "best friend." I wanted others to believe that me and the "Big Guy Upstairs" had something special going on.

Crossing my fingers, and with much enthusiasm, I'd tell people, "Me and God are like this! We're tight like that!"

Then those listening would be like,
"Man, I wish me and God were like that, too!"

It's so nice to be admired.

. . .

During my early days of college, I read a profound
quote by A.W. Tozer which stuck with me ever since:

*What comes into your mind when you think about
God is the most important thing about you.*[2]

My thoughts about God are the most important thing
about me? Do they really matter that much?

Well, looking back on my life, and remembering some
of my lonely "experiences" with the God I believed
in, I guess my thoughts really did matter. My beliefs
did affect my life in significant ways. Which is why,
in recent years, I started to wonder if God is really
"out there."

I mean, if God really is "out there," then *Who* or *What*
is *He/She/It* like? Is it possible to even "personally"
know this God—let alone describe him/her/it?

We all have our own names for God, don't we?
Some call God:

Jesus,
Universe,
Source Energy,
Higher Power,
Spirit,
Big Guy in the Sky,
Or (if you're an atheist) "a joke."

But no matter what name we assign to God, in my opinion, it's still ...
*just a name.*

To be honest, I don't even think we should be fighting over which name is the absolute, and only correct name, to use for God. I know that might offend some religious folks. People can stick to whatever name they want to use for all I care. Because to me, whatever name is used is still limited to the *meaning* we pour into it.

For instance, what about the label *Christian*? When some people hear this religious label, they automatically assume all Christians are: narrow-minded, judgmental, ignorant, or anti-intellectual. Maybe some are. But this perception shouldn't apply to all Christians.

Or what about when people hear my name? For some, they automatically think: heretic, false teacher, unorthodox, or even extreme. Others, however, think of: friend, brother, teacher, or husband (of course, this one applies only to my wife).

You see, that's my point. The meaning we pour into the names and labels is up for debate. Some can be true and some can be false. But all names—even if they're true—have *limitations*. They shouldn't totally define me or anyone else.

I think the same goes for "God" as well. Any name we call "God" will always fall short because of our limited understanding.

• • •

No one has GOD all figured out. No one. I find it silly when I meet religious folks who talk like they do. Just because people have theological degrees or letters behind their name doesn't always mean much.

Personally, I don't think any generation has fully "arrived" concerning our understanding of God. We all have our "blind spots"—including myself—which I think future generations will eventually see and criticize.

Our "knowledge" of God is many times shaped by our own *experiences*. So, unless we look within, how can we even go beyond them?

In the Bible, God is described as having arms, eyes, and even a face. God is also described as Mother,

Father, an animal, and inanimate objects like a rock or a fortress.

Are they true? Sure. Although, it depends on what we mean. Could it be that these are simply descriptions of the many ways people have experienced God to be like?

Here's what I think we've done as humans. We generally take our good qualities—like love, power, and knowledge—and we add the prefix *omni* to them to describe God. You can't really blame us though. After all, perceptions of God are simply human interpretations. None of us can get beyond that. It's all we can do, really.

That being said, God usually seems to
*look* like us,
*talk* like us,
and even *act* like us.

For instance, if we're angry, then God is angry.
If we're judgmental, then God is judgmental.
If we're racist and exclusive, then God is racist and exclusive.

But if we think God only looks, talks, or acts the way as understood by one person or religion, then you know what?

*We might actually miss him*
*if he walked right by us.*

Words, images, and doctrines can't *totally* define God. They can't. They merely try to explain God—in ways for us to understand and relate on a human level. But in the end, language ultimately fails to capture the true essence of who (or what) God is. Which is why, these days, I hesitate to dogmatically say,

"God *is* ... (Fill in the blank)."

I'd want to qualify it first by saying, "I believe," before giving any definition.

Sure, I believe "God is love." We all want to believe that. I think we can apprehend that statement to some degree. But, still, can't we admit, we're all *experientially* learning what love is? I know I am in certain areas of my life.

But go for it. Try it. Explain "God" to someone.
What words would you use?

Here's what I think would happen.

You'd be off to a good start. Then, in the middle of your explanation,
you'd be like, "... bleh ..."

You'd be dumbfounded. You'd be, well, at a loss for words. And you know what?

Me, too.

What makes us think we can *totally* define God in a word, a phrase, or even a sentence? Even the word "God" needs defining for goodness sake. What makes us think that we, with our finite understanding, can limit an infinite God to a single word? I bet if you ask ten people to explain the word "God" to you, then guess what? You'll most likely get ten different answers.

What makes us think we can make God fit nicely and neatly in our limited theological boxes?

*I believe God will smash any theological box, any day, and any time.*

*For real.*

• • •

I'm not sure if you've noticed this, but God has been through somewhat of a makeover (an evolution if you will) throughout history. Don't get me wrong, I don't really mean that God changes (maybe God does, who knows?), but rather our *perceptions* of God have changed. It's undeniable.

Think about it for a moment. Go back as far as you can in history and notice how many people perceived God. To them, God was tribal, angry, sexist, and violent.

Sadly, some 21st century Christians have not let go of that primitive, archaic way of understanding God. They've taken steps backward to a less informed and enlightened time and still believe God to be that way. And look at how much damage that's done to society.

Thankfully, more and more people are moving away from *that* version of God. It's a distorted view, which must be done away with, or Christianity won't survive in an ever-changing and progressive world. Leaving behind these disturbing images of God has, in my opinion, made this world a better place.

Sure, although crap still happens around the world, I believe all the evil atrocities committed in the name of God were based on *that* version of God.

I love what my friend, Darin Hufford, says,
"Whatever we believe about love,
we believe about God."[3]

So true. If we believe God's love is tribal, angry, sexist, and violent, then guess how we'll end up behaving? We could literally justify anything—no matter how evil it is—and say, "Hey, at least God has my back!"

So it's all based on *perception*. I know we're all learning. But which perceptions are creating a better world?

• • •

As a student of theology and philosophy, I've spent years studying the arguments for the existence of God. I've spoken at events, debated with atheists, and evangelized the "unsaved," trying to prove the existence of an *external* being beyond us.

God, for me, was the "highest being" who had to be proved. Why? Because, for some reason, my version of God at that time wasn't obvious to people.

I remember hearing a "worship leader" (I'm not too fond of that title)[4] answer the question of why they led the congregation in song, which I find to be problematic.

"We praise and worship God to draw his presence," he said.

You see, for him (and many others),
God is "out there" and distant.
God is an object we love *outside* of ourselves.
God is *external* to everyday life and human activity.
God is "up in the sky" looking down, only willing to be present among those who satisfy his narcissistic longings. (We need to *first* tell God how awesome he

is in order for him to respond and be in our midst.)

This mindset has created for a lot of people, including myself in the past, a feeling that God is "far away" unless we do something "religious."

Supposedly,
God is not "with us,"
unless we pray,
unless we ask,
or unless we do something "spiritual."

Now, I know what I'm about to say might sound strange—especially coming from a guy who spent years studying and "proving" the existence of God.

But I believe we should start moving away from all these debates "proving" the existence of a God who is "out there."

Because, as I already mentioned, I no longer believe God is "out there."

It doesn't make sense to me anymore.

I don't believe God to be a deity apart (separate) from us.
I don't even believe God to be the "highest being" among beings.

Rather,
I believe God is the *ground* of all that is.[5]
I believe God is the infinite *center* of life.

I don't think God is some distant creator who happens to intervene in human affairs whenever he feels like it. No, I believe God is found in the very *depths of humanity*—the very *core* of all that is.

Maybe God isn't simply this invisible best friend "up in the sky" who only talks to you with an audible voice.

Maybe the issue is whether or not we can *discover* God in every aspect of human life.

What if God is a lot closer to us than we think?

What if God is not simply present in only the "spiritual" activities we do, but in the exciting and the "mundane"?

What if God is this inescapable presence *beneath*, *above*, and *in* all things—and the only issue is whether or not we are able to "see"?[6]

What if God is the very air we breathe and the life-force we experience?

What if God is not some external object of our love,

but instead, is both the *source* and *manifestation* of love itself?

And what if, as I'm typing, I'm still having a hard time explaining who or what God is? (Oh no ... it's happening.)

Well, let me keep trying.

Bleh ...

• • •

I once heard someone say:
*We don't have to believe in God*
*in order to experience him.*
(Read this over again and let it sink in a bit.)

That's deep. And I also happen to think it's true.

Do you have to intellectually believe in God in order to experience the *excitement* of the birth of your child?

Do you have to intellectually believe in God in order to experience the *comfort* of a hug?

Do you have to intellectually believe in God in order to experience the *encouragement* of a friend?

I believe God is the *source*
of all those precious moments.

You may be wondering, "So then, who or what exactly
is *God*?" Would you like me to give a complete and
precise definition?

Well, I ... just ... can't.

• • •

I vividly remember a time I was in the college library
using the computer. Out of nowhere, there was an
overwhelming sense of love pouring all over me—
right then and there—as I was typing away at the
keyboard. I couldn't contain the emotions. It was so
powerful that I had to get out of my seat and go to
the stairwell, because I couldn't stop crying. Love, at
that moment, flooded my soul.

It was real. Tangible. Overwhelming.

I don't think God "showed up" at that moment. And I
don't think God decided to love me more at that moment either. I believe God's love for me is constant
and unchanging.

But one thing is certain: *I was aware.*

I'm not saying being aware of Presence always leads

to an experience like this. We all respond to love in different ways at different times.

Sometimes awareness leads to the feeling of ...
joy,
peace,
or hope.

Whatever you experience, it'll all be rooted in love.

• • •

I want you to stop for a moment after reading this paragraph. Be still. Be present. Do it for about fifteen seconds. And then pay attention to what you *hear*. (Seriously, try it.)[7]

OK, what did you hear? Music? Birds chirping? Cars driving by? Rain falling? Children playing? The wind?

Isn't it interesting that some of those things you heard were most likely there the entire time? It's just that *now* you were simply made *aware* of them.

Now pay attention again. Be still. Be present. Do it for about fifteen seconds. This time pay attention to what you *feel*.

OK, what did you feel?

Your breathing? Sensations in your body? Peace?
Love? Joy? Presence, perhaps?
Can't fully explain it? Exactly.

There's something about being aware of Presence,
which is difficult to explain. It's like ... well ...
...

• • •

Although I don't totally understand all this "God stuff"
at the moment (as if I ever will), these thoughts have
benefitted me in many ways.

Now, more than ever,
I *see* God in everything—in people, places,
and things.
I *hear* God's voice in many ways—not limited
to words being spoken.
And I *feel* God's presence—even in the simplest
moments in life.

You see, God is present in every moment of our lives
...
when we're playing with kids,
making love,
watching TV,
walking the dog,
or even mowing the lawn.

The question is: Are we *aware*?

Are you aware ...
when walking,
eating food,
changing diapers,
taking out the trash,
or even sitting on the toilet
(where I've received great insights)?

The beautiful truth is that God permeates life.
*All of it.*

And like I already said, I no longer believe God is
"out there."

I believe ...
God is *here*.

TWO

# THE BIBLE:
# THE PAPER GOD

*"...no considerate God would destroy the human mind by making it so rigid and unadaptable as to depend upon one book, the Bible, for all the answers."*
**—ALAN WATTS**

*"My goal is to force Christians to think about what they would believe if the Bible itself was undermined as a source of divine truth."*
**—JOHN LOFTUS**

If the Bible didn't exist, what would you believe?

I know tons of professing Christians who say, because of the Bible, they learned about God's love, a place called heaven, and even how to love their neighbors as they would love themselves.

On the other hand,
I also know of other professing Christians—the more hateful ones (yes, they exist)—who say, because of the Bible, they learned about God's anger, an eternal torture chamber called "hell," and even how we should be violent toward our enemies.

Are Christians reading the same Bible? Well, if they are, I'm guessing each group would accuse the other of misinterpreting the Bible.

What do you think?

What if both groups are right? What if the Bible, properly understood, teaches all of the things I mentioned above? What if, whether we want to admit it or not, the Bible affirms incoherent and sometimes contradictory perspectives?

What if the Bible, should I dare say it,
is wrong on certain issues?

Is it at least *possible*?

Now, if you're already someone who believes it *is* possible for the Bible to be wrong on certain issues, well then, this chapter shouldn't be too much of a stretch for you. In fact, it might even confirm some of your thoughts.

But, if you're someone who believes it is *not* possible for the Bible to be wrong whatsoever, then *why* do you believe that?

Did you find out for yourself?
Is it a leap of faith?
Did somebody tell you it's true and you simply ended up "believing" it? (This is what happened to me.)

Before you start thinking I might dismiss the Bible completely and consider it pure fairy-tale, let me give you a little bit of my background.

• • •

I'd be lying if I told you I read the Bible everyday. I don't. But I used to. For years, I read it everyday of the week. It was something I was proud to do as a Christian. It was like wearing a badge of honor letting everyone know how "spiritual" I was.

But I have to admit, guilt and religious obligation were sometimes the driving force to read my Bible. Sure, I'd sometimes read it because "I wanted to know God" and all. But for the most part, I would read because, as a Christian, I was "supposed to."

To add even more pressure, I also read the Bible because I was a pastor. *Crap. I guess I definitely had no excuse then.*

My friends and family encouraged me to read and meditate on the Bible day and night—to hear God's voice through these special pages. It was ultimately through this book, and by the guidance of the Holy Spirit, that I would figure out "God's will" for my life. And who would want to miss out on that?
I sure didn't.

So I read it.
Several times.
Over and over again.

I experienced a whole range of emotions when I read the Bible.

There were times ...
I was moved to tears because a verse
"spoke to me."
I received insight and wisdom.
I was inspired to love.
I felt challenged.
I felt guilty.
I felt confused.

I felt indifferent and just didn't "give a rip."
And, yes, there were even times I was simply
bored out of my mind.

As you can see, some of my experiences were good.
And other times they were ... well ... not so good.

Whatever I experienced during those times, I was
usually driven by the idea that I was supposed to
read it—no matter what.

Why?

Because it was the "Christian thing" to do.
And it was God's "primary" way of speaking to me.

But here's what I wondered throughout the years. If
the Bible is such a wonderful book—in its *entirety* (I
have to emphasize this), then why was it so difficult
for me to "get into it"?

Was *I* the problem? Or was the *Bible* the problem?
*Both*? Or could it be that the Christian subculture
has placed unrealistic expectations of the Bible on
people?

For instance,
I was told the Bible has "the answer to everything."
Now, that's a bold statement. But is it true?

For years—although I never wanted to admit it—I actually enjoyed reading other Christian books more (and felt guilty for doing so) than the Bible itself. After all, they were easier to understand. Not to mention, I'm also the type who loves the "cliff notes" version of books anyway.

I used to think, "Crap, is it really wrong to not have the Bible as #1 in my *favorite books* section on all my social media profiles?" (Remember, I was a pastor.)

• • •

To many Christians, the Bible is not just any book. It's *The Book*—the "book of all books," if you will. It transcends culture and time. And it's superior to every other religious book out there, too.

So we're told.

The Bible is considered to be the divine manual for living—"God's Word" itself.

Do you want to know about dating?
Look to the Bible.
Do you want to know about sex?
Look to the Bible.
Do you want to know about marriage?
Look to the Bible.

Whatever questions are floating around in that thinking-brain of yours, look no further for the answer.

Because ... supposedly ... *every* answer you need is found in the Bible.

Now if you think that's a big claim, well, here's another one that many Christians dogmatically make:

*The Bible (or at least the original manuscripts) is without error.*

The fancy word for this is *inerrancy*. This means the Bible is completely true in areas of science, history, theology—basically in everything it claims.

But, according to inerrantists (those who hold to inerrancy), that's not what makes the Bible so special. There's more to it. Other books contain truth as well, don't they? But the Bible, it is claimed, is still on another level.

You see, not only is the Bible true, but it's also *divinely authoritative.*

Why?

Because it's "from God." All of it.

And the God of the Bible "don't make no mistakes."

Supposedly.
So we're told.

• • •

During my speaking engagements, I often get asked whether or not the Bible is true.

Here's how I usually interact with the audience:

Me: How many of you have read the Bible from cover to cover?

Audience: (A few hands go up, while the majority of the hands stay down.)

Me: OK. Isn't it true that some of you who have not read the entire Bible from cover to cover still *assume* it's all completely true?

Audience: (Smiles of embarrassment on people's faces.)

Me: So then why do you do that?

Audience: (Still smiling.)

Me: Now, for those of you who have read the Bible from cover to cover, can you honestly say that you've made sure that every single verse in the Bible is true?

Audience: (Some smiling. Some looks of guilt.)

Me: I doubt it. Yet some of you still assume it's 100% true and inerrant.

Think about it, folks. It's all *ASSUMED!*

Now, we all know what "assumptions" make us out to be, right? It makes an ...

Never mind, I won't even go there.

• • •

Whether or not you believe the Bible is completely true is not the main issue I have. For me, what it comes down to is whether or not you're being completely honest with yourself (and others) with what you claim to believe.

You see, throughout the years I've read hundreds of books trying to prove the Bible is true. And to be honest, I actually read them to *confirm* my already-made assumption. The authors of these books would bust out historical evidence, philosophical reasoning, and theological arguments at their disposal.

Pretty impressive.

To justify the Bible, they'd say things like:

"Jesus was a real person."
"The crucifixion really happened."
"Messianic prophecies were fulfilled."

I get it. I don't deny there's truth to be found in the Bible. But when you get down to the nitty-gritty, is *everything* in the Bible true?

The sweeping statement, "Everything in the Bible is true," which religious folks love to make has to, in my opinion, sweep a whole lot of things under the rug in order to avoid some major criticisms.

Hear me out on this. What if everything the Bible affirms is not true? What if it's not simply our interpretations, which could possibly be wrong, but what if the *authors of Scripture* themselves got some things wrong?

Yes, I know. It can be a scary thought for some of us. I know those with a more "liberal" bent are probably thinking, "What's the big deal? I never thought it was all true anyway."

But I know for many fundamentalists (and I've been there), it's supposedly the foundation for *everything* they claim to believe. So questioning its truthfulness is a pretty big deal.

Here's something really important to consider:

What if a person's belief in the authority and inerrancy of the Bible can be undermined? What if the Bible can no longer be demonstrated as the *ultimate standard* for truth for every matter in life?

What then?

Before I even explored this possibility
I used to think:

*Nah! I won't even go there.*
*I wouldn't know what to believe anymore.*
*I need some sort of standard to live by.*
*Plus, the people I respect and admire*
*believe the entire Bible is true.*
*And they're a lot smarter than me.*
*So who am I to question?*

But in recent years, a shift happened in me. And after this "shift hit the fan," I haven't looked at the Bible the same way since.

In fact, once a person's belief in inerrancy is undermined, and once the Bible is no longer considered the ultimate standard of truth, then a person's approach and interpretation of Scripture become a whole new ball game.

• • •

Let me make myself clear on this.  As you continue reading, you might think, "Josh, why are you trying to make the Bible look so bad?"

But that's not my end goal.
We've just made the Bible look *too good*.

There are more than enough books written which highlight the good parts of the Bible. But to be straight up with you, this chapter isn't one of them.

Although I appreciate the Bible for the many treasures it contains, I want to *emphasize* certain parts of the Bible, which I find to be problematic. Why? Because they've been *de-emphasized* (or ignored completely) by many religious folks who are trying to protect "God's Word" from being criticized.

And, in my opinion, I don't think many leaders within mainstream Christianity have dealt with these problematic passages adequately.

The rest of this chapter might piss some of you off (if you're not already). But, hey, it may liberate others. Or it might even confirm what some of you already know and believe.

Keep reading at your own risk.

• • •

Imagine you're with a group of friends and family discussing a very important issue—let's say, homosexuality, for example. A committed, Bible-believing Christian walks through the door and "wants in" on the discussion.

He interrupts and comments,
"I'm glad you're all thinking through this very important topic. But what does God think about homosexuality? Because, ultimately, it doesn't matter what any of us think. What it comes down to is what the Bible says. And the Bible says ..."

Afterward he cites several verses from the Bible and makes his theological case.

In other words, his mentality is basically this:
*The Bible said, I believe it, that settles it.*

Doesn't this mentality shut down conversations?
Doesn't this mentality say,
"Who cares what you think"?
Doesn't this mentality say,
"Don't think. Let the Bible think for you"?

Sure, ultimately opinions don't matter. Truth matters. But if our opinions don't matter, then why should we trust *all* the opinions of the authors of the Bible? Why make them the exception?

How do we know if everything they believed and affirmed is true?

• • •

I once heard a preacher describe the Bible using an acronym. It goes something like this:

**B**asic
**I**nstructions
**B**efore
**L**eaving
**E**arth

Pretty clever, isn't it? But basic? The Bible? Hmmm ...

Try telling that to the tens of thousands of Christian denominations and "fringe" groups around the world who divide over these "basic" instructions.

Try telling that to the readers who have a difficult time understanding the "hard sayings" of Jesus.

Try telling that to the readers who just "don't get" some of the parables.

Try telling that to the readers who simply have no clue on how to interpret the apocalyptic language found in the book of the Revelation.

Or maybe we're just not "spiritual" enough to understand this basic book?

Maybe we're using too much mind?
Maybe we're using too much heart?
Maybe we don't have enough
Holy Spirit illumination?
Maybe we have bad translations?

*There are just too many stinkin' "maybes"!*

Trust me, I've had my share of searching the Bible
for answers—especially during difficult times in my
life. I remember when I'd ask God a question, close
my eyes, open up my Bible at random, point to a
particular spot on a page with my finger, and then
I'd magically get my answer.

Sometimes my answer would be a punctuation mark,
or the white space between the lines, or even Bible
verses which seemed to have no connection whatsoever to my question. (At least I tried to make sense
of them to make myself feel better.)

I bet I'm not the only one who's done this "lucky-
dipping" method either. I'm sure a lot of people have.
And don't get me wrong, I bet there were (and are)
times when God actually did (and does) speak to
people in this "random" way.

But we need to ask ourselves: Why the heck do so many of us do this? Why do we put so much pressure on ourselves to hear from God through this book?

• • •

I've heard a lot of clichés about the Bible. I'm sure you have, too. I sometimes wonder if the people who repeatedly say them even believe what they're saying.

Here are a few, which I'm sure you've heard at one time or another. I also include my short responses:

*1. The Bible is alive!*

Me: I'm sure it is—in a certain way. "God-breathed" maybe? Sure, it can inspire us. But I sometimes wonder if we enjoy the notes, articles, commentaries, and all the add-ons in the Bible more than the actual Bible itself at times.

*2. You can't pick and choose what you want to believe and follow in the Bible.*

Me: Says who? Of course I can. We all do this with pretty much every book we read. What makes the Bible the exception? Many Christians today say and do things, which go beyond (and even contradict) the Bible itself. Notice a lot has changed since the first century.

3. *Everything has to be in the Bible
   or else it's not true.*

Me: That statement itself is not found in the Bible. The word "Bible" is not found in the Bible. The words "rapture" and "Trinity" are not found in the Bible. And this may be a shocker to you as well, but the "sinner's prayer" isn't even found in the Bible.

4. *The Bible records evil doings of people, not God.*

Me: Please, read it again. Especially the Old Testament.

5. *The Bible is a love letter.*

Me: Are stories of murder, rape, incest, genocide, infanticide, child-sacrifice, racism, polygamy, adultery, deception, and idolatry—which are found in the pages of Scripture—part of the love letter, too?

6. *Everything in the Bible points to Jesus.*

Me: Hmmm ... but why do so many of the violent passages in the Bible contradict the life and teachings of the non-violent Jesus?

7. *Our experiences should never define the Bible,
   rather the Bible should define our experiences.*

Me: Isn't the Bible based on people's experiences?

Which Bible defined the author's experiences? And what about all the countless experiences people have today which are not found in the Bible? Are they all unreliable and invalid?

*8. The Bible says it. I believe it. That settles it.*

Me: Or is it more like, "The Bible said it. You *interpreted* it. That settles it"?

*9. God preserved His Word from containing mistakes.*

Me: That's an assumption. If that's true, then why doesn't God preserve the right interpretation of the Bible to make things easier for us?
(Of course, some will argue he has, as long as it's *their* interpretation.)

*10. The Bible is authoritative.*

Me: Isn't any book which contains truth authoritative in a sense? Truth is truth, right? The Bible, after all, is compiled of sixty-six books (the Protestant canon) from several authors and was not written in *one single unified voice.* (Any honest reader can admit this.) So to be more realistic, whenever truth is discovered, shouldn't it be accepted? And whenever falsehood is discovered, shouldn't it be rejected? We do this with every other book, don't we?

*11. The Bible is true because
the Bible itself affirms it.*

Me: So the Bible is true because the Bible says it's true? (Try saying that again out loud without smiling.) How would you feel if a Muslim used that same logic to justify the reliability of the Qur'an?

*12. If any part of the Bible is not true,
then how can you trust any of it?*

Me: Have you ever read a book where you didn't agree with a chapter, but you loved the rest of the book? Or did you throw it all out? No need to "throw the baby out with the bathwater." We all have things to learn. And so did many of the authors of the Bible.

• • •

Do you have friends who constantly pull out the "God told me" card? I know I have. In fact, I've even been guilty of it myself in the past.

Do these sound familiar to you?

"God told me to marry you."
"God told me to break up with you."
"God told me you're wrong."
"God told me that I'm called to go to Africa."

I find it interesting when I meet Christians who say they constantly struggle with hearing God's voice, yet they hear God ever so clearly when they want to marry someone.

Now don't get me wrong, I totally believe God speaks to people. But can very sincere people be mistaken when it comes to hearing God's voice?

Of course. We all know that.

So why the *exception* for the authors of the Bible? Why can't they be mistaken at times? Who says that when they said, "God said," it's really God?

I mean, I've even heard many Christians teach that we are under something called a New Covenant of Grace, which, according to them, means we have a *superior revelation* to those under the Old Covenant of Law.

Based on that understanding, don't we, who are under the New Covenant, *still* make mistakes when we think, write, and speak on what are sometimes called "spiritual matters"?

The obvious answer is: *yes.*

Then why is it so hard for some of us to accept the possibility of the Old and New Testament writers being mistaken at times as well? Were they not human? Did God possess their bodies and control their hands as they wrote things down?

Of course not.

They were *inspired*. (Not forced.)

I've been inspired before. You've been inspired before, I'm sure. Yet we've all made mistakes.
And we *still* do.

Just like us,
the authors of the Bible were people of their times.
Just like us, they were limited by their culture.
Just like us, they had their own worldview.

And just like us, sometimes they got things right.
And just like us, sometimes they got things wrong.

*Surprise, surprise.*

• • •

As for the "sweeping things under the rug" comment I made earlier in this chapter, here's what I mean. Read the Old Testament especially.

God makes Hitler look like Mother Teresa.
I'm not kidding.

There's a *dark side* of God which many religious folks don't like mentioning. Chances are, you already know about it.

But here's the thing:

We've been *trained* not to see this dark side of God.
We've been *persuaded* to deny the obvious.

You see, pastors, theologians, and teachers have come up with clever ways to get Christians to *ignore* this dark side. But what's even more disturbing is the more clever ones have gotten people to actually *justify* this dark side of God.

Here's what Raymund Schwager, a man who is willing to acknowledge the obvious when reading the Bible, has to say:

> The theme of God's bloody vengeance occurs in the Old Testament even more frequently than the problem of human violence. Approximately one thousand passages speak of Yahweh's blazing anger, of his punishments by death and destruction, and how like a consuming fire he passes judgment, takes revenge, and threatens annihilation.... No other topic is as often mentioned as God's bloody works.[1]

God's bloody vengeance? One thousand passages?

Yup. It's right there in the Bible.

But you don't have to take my word for it. Do yourself a favor and find out for yourself (if you haven't already).

In the meantime, I have a couple questions to ask.

If the Bible is true in everything it affirms,[2] how can anyone trust the portrayal of a God who ...
condones slavery,[3]
sends plagues,[4]
commands genocide and infanticide,[5]
sends a worldwide flood killing most of humanity,[6]
sends an evil and lying spirit to torment someone,[7]
forces parents to eat their own children,[8]
asks a faithful servant to sacrifice his own child as a test,[9]
and who is said to be the author of evil?[10]

Should I keep going? Sadly, there's more. And no, I didn't just describe "the devil" either.

This is the God found throughout the Bible who many claim is supposedly "good." And because this God is supposedly "good," it's believed that these acts of God are good as well.

*Dude, what are some religious folks smoking?*

You'd have to do a bunch of hermeneutical gymnastics to explain these babies away. You'd have to flip, contort, distort, or whatever, to justify *all* of the disturbing passages I just mentioned as good.

Now let's make it up close and personal.

What if, by the command of God, *you* were:
to become a slave,
forced to eat your own child,
have your ethnic group "utterly destroyed,"
or have your precious child sacrificed?

Would you be OK with that?
Or were these things OK back then but wrong today?
If so, I thought, "God never changes."[11]

Oh no, confusing.

• • •

I'll never forget the time I sat in the backseat of my friend's car with his child. I happened to notice a children's book about Noah's Ark lying there. Nothing was special about it. I'd seen a bunch of these kinds of books.

But this time was different.

For years I focused on the ark and how God spared Noah and his family during the flood. But this time, I saw it from another angle.

Yes, a family was spared.

But (and it's a big BUT) *God literally wiped out and killed the rest of humanity by drowning them.*

(Read the last line again slowly. If it doesn't make you question even just a little bit, then I don't know what will.)

I'm sure some will come to the Bible's defense and say, "But the people of the world at that time were evil. They deserved it." (By the way, Noah and his family weren't necessarily saints either. Don't believe me? Then read the story.)[12]

This brings to mind a story, which my family loves to tell people, especially when we're near any type of swimming pool.

Let me be the first to admit that as a kid, I was a rascal. My close friends growing up said there was a movie made about me called *Problem Child* (1990). (The title says it all.) Of course, my friends were joking (sort of). You see, I fought with my parents a lot. I even cussed at them. I mean, I didn't just say words like *shoot* or *crap*. I said the real "bad" words—the kind that makes a mother wash her kid's mouth out with soap—which is literally what my mother did to me one time.

Not only was I a problem at home, but I used to cause a lot of trouble on the streets as well. I used to get into fights. I used to steal. And I'd give my parents unnecessary headaches.

OK, back to my main point. (I needed to give a little background first.) When I was a kid, I fell into my cousin's swimming pool. Unlucky me, I didn't know how to swim. So who came to my rescue? Supermom! (Who, by the way, also didn't know how to swim. Thank God the pool was shallow.)

Now, think about it. When I fell into the pool my mom could've thought, "Hmmm ... well, Josh is such a bad kid. I think I'll just leave him there to drown. I think he deserves it."

No way!

No matter how "bad" I was, my mom loved me. And this love compelled her to jump into the pool and save me. Not only that, thankfully, she even gave me a chance to grow up and change for the better.

"Josh," you might say, "you were just a kid. Of course your mom wouldn't drown you on purpose."

Yes, that's my point.

Now try telling that to all the children (aside from Noah's) throughout the entire world who were killed by the flood sent by God. (I know you can't tell dead children anything, but I think you know what I mean.)

Did *all* the children during the flood deserve to die? What about the unborn babies? They didn't do "jack squat." Or what about the children who were mentally retarded?

Still, some might defend the flood and say, "Well, God probably knew those kids and unborn babies would've grown up to be murderers anyway."

Maybe. But if God operates like that, then why didn't God just get rid of Hitler, or Stalin, or some other crazy dictator during their childhood before they grew up to kill millions of innocent people who, by the way, didn't deserve it?

Consider the deaths caused by tsunamis.

*If* they are caused by God as judgment, as some religious folks claim, then why do they end up killing the "not so bad" people? Does God have really bad aiming skills?

Or what about the 9/11 attacks in New York?

Some of you were actually there when it happened. Or some of you, like me, watched it on television wondering if you were watching a movie.

It was surreal.
It was painful.
It was traumatic.
It was unforgettable.

It was ... a judgment from God?

Sad to say, I literally know some religious folks who do believe 9/11 was an act of God's judgment. They claim a holy God did what he did because of all the sin and evil of the American people.

But if you're like most people, you probably think what happened that day wasn't an act of God. In fact, some of you might've even wondered where God was on that tragic day.

Here's the scary thing though, you can actually *justify* what happened on 9/11 using—you guessed it—the Bible.

Some will say, "No, you could only justify 9/11 when you take the Bible out of context."

To those sincerely good people who would say such a thing, I have this to say to you:

*Read the Bible again. Carefully.*

I'm not against recording the bad parts of a story either. A story is a story. But what's so messed up is that some of the most violent moments recorded in these Bible stories were supposedly *caused by God.*

Did you catch that?
*By God.*

But like I already said, many Christians have either turned a blind eye, or have come up with clever ways to justify God's "apparent" evils.

What do we do with the conquest narratives where God orders the Israelites to invade foreign lands and completely destroy them?[13]

It's right there in the Bible.

Thing is, there are always two sides to every story, right? I wonder how those who were attacked by "God's people" would've described those violent events from *their* perspective if they survived.

But you know what? We will never know.

Remember ... *it's the winners who write history.*
(If it is history.)

• • •

Whenever I bring up this whole issue of violence in the Bible, some people become uncomfortable. Some even get pissed-off at me for questioning "God's Word." Then there are those who tell me I need to read those violent stories with "spiritual eyes."

"Spiritual eyes"? What does that even mean?

So when *people* do bad stuff in the Bible, it's considered bad, right? But when *God* does bad stuff in the Bible, it's considered good? Am I missing something here?

Oh, and people just love pulling out the "it's all a mystery" card.

For instance, they read something good in the Bible and give credit to God. Then they read something caused by God, which is obviously bad, and plead mystery.

Huh?

They say things like, "We are finite. God is infinite. God is good. His ways are above our ways. His thoughts are higher than our thoughts. It's all a mystery."

But here's a thought:

If all appearances of "evil" are a mystery, then how can we call any of God's ways good? After all, they are *mysterious*, right?

Yes, I'm finite.
But I'm not stupid.

• • •

This is where the term "biblical" begins to have its problems for me. Should a Christian's goal be to live "biblically"? If so, what does it even mean?

Isn't calling down "fire and brimstone" to fall upon all the evil, violent, and homosexual people in San Francisco and Los Angeles "biblical"?

Isn't genocide and infanticide "biblical"?

Do you have children? Well, the Bible gives some painful advice: "Happy is the one who seizes your infants and dashes them against the rocks."[14]

*Say what?!*

Do you believe in the afterlife? Sorry to burst your bubble, but according to Ecclesiastes 9:2-10, there is no afterlife.

Are you a woman gifted in teaching and leadership?

Well, if you are, I'm sorry about that, too.

According to 1 Tim 2:12–14 (NIV) it says, "I do not permit a woman to teach or to assume authority over a man; she must be quiet. For Adam was formed first, then Eve. And Adam was not the one deceived; it was the woman who was deceived and became a sinner."

Is the author of 1 Timothy making a "cultural" argument as many commentators claim? Nope. The argument is clear and simple:

Man was created first.
Woman was deceived first.

There's nothing "cultural" about that.

Does your particular ethnic group have a history of slavery? Well, surprisingly, not only does the Old Testament not condemn slavery, the New Testament doesn't either.[15]

And here's the irony of it all. In the same Bible, I can point out other verses, which imply the *opposite* of these disturbing verses I just mentioned.[16]

But if every single verse in the Bible—every jot and tittle—is supposed to carry equal weight, as inerrantists say, *then by golly, the Bible is stinkin' confusing.*

And get this, if one—just one—verse in the Bible is found not to be true, then guess what?

*Inerrancy collapses.*

. . .

I find it interesting that so many Christians believe the Bible was written by One Divine Author: God.

But why would it be?
Think about it.

It contains sixty-six books.
It contains a variety of different literary genres.
It's written by dozens of different authors with diverse backgrounds.
And it was written over a span of 1,500 years.

So based on these facts, what makes us think the Bible should be entirely consistent? Is it really difficult to believe that a compilation of religious books can contradict one another? It happens a lot even today, doesn't it?

When you read the Bible, honestly that is, it's obvious that it's written in a *number of voices* and not just one. These voices express themselves with their cultural perspectives and time-bound limitations.

That said, doesn't the word "biblical" become problematic?

The term "biblical" assumes it's written in one voice by One Divine Mind. It assumes every single author in the Bible is agreeing with each other.
But putting all assumptions aside, we know that's not true.

Think of it like this: Do authors sometimes revise their books? Some do. Why? Because aside from wanting to simply add more content, it's also because their views have changed since the first edition was written.

So why can't we think the same goes for the authors of the Bible as well?

Could they have been mistaken, in certain ways, about God, the world, and life? (Remember, I'm not saying *everything* they believed was wrong.)

Could *any* part of their writings be wrong?
Isn't it at least *possible*?

Could it be possible that "God's people" had similar beliefs with their ancient Near Eastern neighbors?

Could it be possible that the practices of human sacrifices, slavery, and polygamy were simply part of their worldview at the time?

Could it be possible that the beliefs in many gods, God (or gods) giving victory in battles, or God controlling "natural" disasters such as famines, earthquakes, and floods were also part of their worldview?

Could it be possible that the sexist attitude, in both the Old and New Testament, was another part of this ancient worldview?

It's definitely possible. And to me, it's highly probable.

So why should we believe everything the authors and characters of the Bible assumed in their worldview was true?

Haven't we outgrown some of their beliefs and practices?

• • •

Now, I know this is lot to "take in" for some of you. And you know what? It's OK. It took me years to get to this point of honesty in my life.

But no matter what your stance is on this topic, don't be afraid to question. And definitely don't be afraid to be honest with yourself.

I guess the billion-dollar question now is: "*How* should we read the Bible?"

I think activist and author Brian McLaren makes a good point in his book *A New Kind of Christianity* when he talks about how we can approach the Bible.[17]

According to McLaren, we can either read the Bible as a *legal constitution* or as a *library*.

For instance, if we read the Bible as a constitution, we can spew out a bunch of Bible verses to get someone to agree with us.

On the other hand, if we read it as a library, we can see it as a collection of different genres—with different voices and perspectives.

So how do we engage with this library and discover which parts are true?
Well, you can ask these questions:

Does it match up with reality?
Is it historically reliable?
Logically consistent?
Is it moral or immoral?
Culture-bound or relevant for today?
Consistent with love?

It's easy to recognize a progression going on in the Bible—not necessarily in God's character—but in *humanity's understanding.*

In other words,
one author added to the conversation.
Then another added to the conversation.
Then another added to the conversation.
And so on.

And now there's *us*—here and now.
Is it safe to say that we could be *another voice*
to add to the conversation?

Because like the characters in the Bible, aren't we, in
our day and age, constantly learning, growing, and
discovering as well?

We must work through it one text at a time and stop
making sweeping statements about the Bible without
doing our own research. Yes, we're all limited, but we
must try to be as objective as possible.

That said, we can gain a lot of wisdom from the Bible.
We can follow the examples of those who inspire us.
We can even learn from their mistakes. So shouldn't
it be healthy to look *beyond* the authors' limited perspectives as well?

• • •

Imagine with me for moment. What if you were stuck
on an island with no access to a Bible? And let's say
you sucked at memorizing Bible verses, would you
still be OK "spiritually"? Would God stop speaking to

you? Or is God's voice limited to an ancient book? Think of it another way. If someone you love wrote you a letter and you lost it, would you have no chance whatsoever of still getting to know the person? Or if you started speaking out loud to God, in desperate need of help, would God be silent without a Bible to communicate with?

I guess my concern is for those who commit something called "bibliolatry"—the worship of the ...
Father,
Son,
and Holy *Scriptures.*

If God's communication is limited to a book, then just how big is this God? No doubt, it's possible for God to speak through the Bible. But of course, the God who created the heavens and the earth also *supersedes* the Bible.

• • •

Some of you might be wondering why I've spent so much time challenging people's perspective about the Bible.

Just so you know, I'm not the type who dwells on the negative very long (no one should), but what I'm about to say here has to be said.

I'm seriously saddened with how people have justified almost every evil under the sun by using the Bible.

We must stop using the Bible to justify ...
racism,
an "us vs. them" mentality,
persecution of homosexuals,
killing people in the name of God,
the subordination of women to men,
and claiming "natural" disasters as judgments from God.

We must never forget that, before the Bible was put together, the disciples of Jesus lived by the Spirit.

The Spirit was *within them.*
The Spirit is *within you.*

God is not done speaking.
God will continue to speak.

Are you listening?
You are God's voice.
You are God's living letter for all to read.

So speak.

THREE

# GRACE: GIVING UP

*"Too many Christians are living in a house of fear and not in the house of love."*
**—BRENNAN MANNING**

*"Grace doesn't depend on suffering to exist. but where there is suffering you will find grace in many facets and colors."*
**—WM. PAUL YOUNG**

For years I *tried* really hard ...
to act like a good Christian,
to imitate Christ,
to love God,
and to avoid sin.

I tried, and tried, and tried, and tried, and tried.
And guess what?

I failed.

So what did I do?

*I gave up trying.*

Let me explain.

Growing up I went to dozens of what are called "evan-gelistic crusades." People go to these events to hear the gospel and to "get saved" (whatever that means). At these events, a preacher usually talks about God's unconditional love, his grace—all that good stuff you need to hear—hoping to win your heart for Christ.

But that's not all. The preacher then pleads for you to respond to the gospel and make Jesus Christ your "personal Lord and Savior" in order to seal the "sal-vation deal."

You are to come to God "just as you are." And it doesn't

matter who you are. You could be a drug-addict, a pedophile, a crook, a modern-day Hitler—you name it, no one is excluded from "receiving God's grace."

If you end up being one who responds to the gospel, you're then asked to come to the front of the stage to make a public declaration of faith for everyone to witness. Once you reach the stage, you're invited to say something called the "sinner's prayer" aloud.

Then, at that very moment, supposedly,
you're "born-again,"
all your sins are forgiven,
and you're on your way to heaven.

It's a pretty good deal I must say.

Then, after this day of "conversion," some people's lives are truly never the same again.

Here's the thing. For some, their lives get *better*.
But for others, however, their lives get *worse*.

Huh?

Throughout the years, I've had many Christians confess to me that they "came to faith" because they heard the message of God's grace and unconditional love—just like the one at the evangelistic crusades. They even claimed to have a "personal and intimate relationship with God." But over time, and without warning, things changed. Their "relationship" with God became ... well ... no longer a "relationship."

It became about *rules*.
It became about *morality*.
It became about *not sinning*.

It was, in short—*behavior modification*.

Now, I don't know about you, but what I've noticed throughout the years is that many Christians tend to be known for what they *don't* do rather than for what they *do*.

They don't cuss.
They don't smoke.
They don't drink alcohol.
And they definitely don't listen to Lady Gaga.

And many of them are pretty damn (oops) proud of it.

I know, I know, not all Christians are like this. But this is the impression many people have of them.

One perfect example is what happened to a friend of mine at our Christian college. She couldn't take it anymore. Couldn't take what, exactly? The "Christian life" that is. She was fed up one day and confessed:

"Josh, I was barely a new Christian when I first came to this school. Things were so good. But then, over time, Christianity became all about rules. 'I can't do this. I can't do that.' I had to join all these 'accountability groups.' I had to share personal stuff with my leader. It was so weird. Things got so legalistic."

And she's not alone. Her experience is definitely not rare among the religious. In fact, for many people including myself, it was all about following God's biblical principles. It was all about pleasing God more. It was all about avoiding "sin." And it was all about feeling guilty for doing anything fun.

The relationship my friend and I (and I'm sure many others) have had with God was definitely one filled with a lot of guilt and shame. For most of my life, I felt like I had to keep tabs on everything I did. I was told that, whenever I committed "sin," these would be the dire consequences:

*I won't hear God's voice.*
*God won't hear any of my prayers.*
*God's hand will be removed from me.*
*I'll break out of fellowship with God.*
*God will be angry with me.*
*God won't bless me.*
*God will punish me.*

Now, forget about all the ghosts in your closet or the monsters under your bed. For goodness sake, God was the one to be afraid of!

It's weird because I claimed God loved me even though I believed he would hurt me if I ever screwed up. My "relationship" with God was ultimately rooted in fear. And come to think of it, how could I truly love someone whom I'm afraid of? *good point*

Trust me, this is not a good mentality for a child (or anybody) to have.

I'll never forget the time I was a kid and took a nap during the day. Once I awoke, I walked around the house to see who was home. Mom and Dad's room was empty. Sister's room was empty. The entire house was empty. Then it hit me.

*Oh my gosh ... the rapture happened! I was "left behind"!* (OK, you can stop laughing now.)

I couldn't stop crying. The fear hit me like a ton of bricks. Sadness swallowed me up inside. It was too late. It was the end of the world. And I wasn't good enough for God to accept me.

I eventually realized it wasn't the end of the world. And, of course, the rapture didn't happen either. Luckily, my family came home.

But what if it was the end of the world? What if God did remove only the "select few"? Would I be good enough? Would I be part of the "frozen chosen"?

These thoughts haunted me daily.

· · ·

At times, "serving God" became more like a chore, not a joy. It was something I "had to" do. I wanted to prove to God how much I loved him. After all, God's own Son, Jesus Christ, "died on the cross for my sins" (this can be a huge guilt motivator). Obeying God's commandments was the least I could do.

Some days I'd "fall into sin" and promise God I'd never fall into it again. Then I'd get up and try to live better. But not too long after, I'd fall again. In fact, sometimes I'd end up worse than before. Of course, I didn't want anyone to know. Why would I risk my "spiritual" reputation? How could I live with people looking down at me?

So what did I—and what do millions of other religious people all over the world—usually do?

I kept it a secret.    sins

I still went to church every Sunday, and I responded to every "altar call."[1] Since I was already "saved,"

I'd rededicate myself to God over and over again—promising myself, "This time will be different. I'll be a better Christian from this day forward."

While things did seem to get better for a short period of time, unfortunately, I would end up, once again, "falling into sin."

More guilt. More shame. More condemnation.
No joke.

Usually during these crappy moments, I wouldn't talk to God for the rest of the day. I couldn't. I was too embarrassed. I mean, God saw everything I did for goodness sake. I was too afraid to hear what he had to say back to me.

So what was my usual routine? I'd sleep off the guilt, hoping it would be gone by the next morning. And if that method didn't work, there was always Plan B: Do good deeds to make up for the bad ones.

It was an endless cycle—a treadmill of guilt, shame, and self-righteous works.

But I was taught, "God is a God of second chances." *And there were always other people worse off than me.* And, boy, did that perspective make me feel better at times!

I'd move on with my life. And, as usual, I'd pull out the ol' *"This time will be different"* spiel.

So I prayed more.
I tithed more.
I fasted more.
I read the Bible more.
I evangelized more.
I did more, and more, and more,
and more, and more.

But still ... it was never enough.

See, this is what religion did to me. Let me qualify the previous statement: This is what *false religion* did to me.

There's another word for this. It's called *legalism*.

Legalism is when we get so focused on "doing"— focusing more on the external rather than the internal. It's when we get so focused on earning God's approval. And it's when we get so focused on our "good" and everybody else's "bad."

In other words, it's not a good place to be in.

• • •

Surprisingly enough, the legalism didn't stop me. Once

I reached college I was even more "serious" about my faith. Correction: I was a frickin' saint—at least I tried to be. Sure, I had my "screw ups" here and there, but I honestly felt like I could've been the poster-boy for young, godly Christian men. I didn't do a lot of the "bad" things I saw other Christians my age doing. No way. I was all about wanting to stay "pure" before a holy and righteous God.

For years I lived in frustration wondering why other Christians didn't live up to God's "standard" of holiness the way I did (or was it my standard?). I constantly compared myself with others and became very critical of people's lives. Even their theology.

In my mid-twenties, my friends and I got heavily involved in the charismatic revival movement. These were usually big gatherings with a lot of "hyping up" and energy involved.

It was all about ...
"contending for more,"
"digging the wells,"
"paying the price,"
and "believing for open heavens."

I would always cry out—from the top of my lungs I might add—for more power and fire from heaven to come down and touch me.

I wanted supernatural encounters with God, because I wanted to impact the nations.

"God is doing a new thing," I'd hear revivalists say over and over again. And what could I say? I wanted to be a part of it.

Yet there was definitely a "price to pay." All those "works" led me into eventual burn-out.

I was tired, frustrated, and confused. Why did I feel like I always had to "prime the pump" and pull God's arm? Do I always have to scream and pray long hours to get God's attention?

Where was God's grace? I mean, I preached "grace" at the pulpit. I claimed to believe in it. I even claimed to be "saved" by it. But the important question is:

*Did I truly understand grace?*

For years I tried earning God's blessings, his approval, and his love. But they were all conditional. All of it.

Something was seriously wrong with my thinking. But, surprisingly, I still wasn't "getting it."

• • •

During my early years of pastoring, I was considered

"radical" by some of my closest peers. People looked up to me because of my passion for "holiness." I wasn't afraid to offend people at the pulpit. At the time, I thought I had more respect for "God's ways" than "man's ways" and wanted others to know I wasn't playing around.

For instance, if I was aware of a "big sin" going on within the congregation then, concerned for God's holiness, I wasn't afraid to "call it out" at the pulpit and preach against it with a passion.

Sunday after Sunday, I was an expert at giving people guilt-trips.

Yes, I wanted people to feel bad. But at the same time, I also wanted people to feel God's love. (They were pretty confusing messages.) I wanted the "sinners" to realize how bad they were so they wouldn't "fall into the hands of an angry God."

But then I noticed something.

The more I focused on "sin" in my sermons, the more it seemed like people were "sinning" more.

I didn't know what the heck was going on. I couldn't understand why some people were getting worse. Were they simply not "cut out" for radical discipleship? Were they not real Christians?

I thought pointing out people's crap was supposed to help them. I mean, my goal was to "wake up" the hypocrites so they'd stop "dragging Jesus' name in the mud." To me, it was either "get right with God" or "stop calling yourself a Christian." Plain and simple.

But the irony of it all, I later realized, is this: The one thing I was against, I actually *empowered*.[2]

Let me explain.

Imagine being in a friend's home who has a ton of books. Let's say there are thousands of books surrounding you. And let's say you're not much of a reader either. Now, imagine breezing through the shelves and not having any interest whatsoever in reading any of the books. But then one of them catches your eye. It looks like a journal. You know you're not supposed to read it, because it probably contains some personal stuff. Sure, you might ignore reading it at first glance. But it's still there, calling your name (if books could talk). Suddenly, a desire to read it stirs up within you even more. You become curious. *Why can't I read it?* You control yourself. But then the desire to read it becomes like an itch you have to scratch.

So you look at the book one more time. Want to guess what happens next?

You know.

• • •

You see, there's something about prohibitions ("do not's") which stir something up within all of us. Tell a kid not to eat a cookie from the cookie jar, and what does he do? Tell a young sixteen-year-old girl not to see her college boyfriend anymore, and what does she do? Tell Christians not to sin anymore, and what do they do?

You know.

One time I saw a video of mentalist/hypnotist Derren Brown doing an experiment with children. The experiment was to leave the children alone with an empty box in a room and see what they'd do with the box. Before Derren left the room, he instructed the children to guard and not to open it. But what the children didn't know was that Derren was secretly watching them from another room.

During the experiment, Derren stated that the negative suggestion, *"Don't look inside the box,"* was designed to "sit heavily on their minds and stroke their curiosity."

It did just that.

The more the children tried not to open the box, the more difficult it was to resist. Now, you don't have to be a rocket scientist to figure out what happened next. It didn't take too long before each child opened the box.

Another funny example was when I lived in the Philippines for several years. (Now, I'm not trying to make the Philippines look bad, but I'm simply sharing what I've seen happen several times which confirms the point I'm making.) Out on the streets I'd see signs in random places along walls, which said, *"Bawal umihi ditto!"* In Tagalog, this means it's forbidden to take a piss in that specific area.

Do you want to guess what I saw almost every time I saw that sign?

You know.

• • •

Just to clarify, the "do not's" don't necessarily *cause* people to make their choices. But the "do not's" can be the beginning of a focus. And when there's a focus, we usually end up getting what we focus on.

Swiss psychotherapist and psychiatrist Carl Jung shared a very insightful truth:

*What you resist persists.*

In other words, stop directing all your energy to what you *don't* want. Because the more you resist and focus on what you don't want, you'll get. Even if you don't want it.

Accept what is.
And shift your focus to what you *do* want.

It's like when you play basketball, do you focus on where you don't want the ball to go? (If you do, don't be surprised if you always end up getting picked last on the team.) No, you focus on where you want the ball to go: through the hoop.

Is it possible the same goes for "sinning"? Is it possible the more one preaches against it—or focuses on it—the more it increases? When you constantly urge someone to not do something, could it be that you're possibly empowering "sin" without even realizing it? Is sin-focused preaching more of a problem than a solution?

It seems to be.

So maybe we shouldn't be surprised if a congregation, which focuses so heavily on sin, results in being swallowed up by the very thing it's trying so hard to avoid.

What do you think?

. . .

The question I had to answer in my life is: *"Why* do I do what I do?" Or to narrow it down even more: Why do I do good? ~~*Question*~~

~~Am I motivated by guilt?~~ Fear? Religious obligation?

Now, I can't say it's for everything I did, but for the most part, I think a lot of the "religious" things I did growing up were rooted in fear and obligation. I "had to" do them because, if I didn't, I thought God wouldn't bless me in return.

Think of it this way. My wife's "love language" is words of encouragement. (Thank God it's not jewelry.)

Imagine I tell my wife on the day of our wedding anniversary that I love her. Touched by my romantic gesture she says, "Aww ... thanks, Josh. Do you mean it?"

I respond,
"Umm, well, not at the moment. But it's something I'm supposed to say because you're my wife. Plus, it's our anniversary. I'd feel like crap if I didn't."

Is this love?

Imagine another scenario where I look into my wife's eyes and tell her I love her. Once again, touched by my romantic gesture she says, "Aww ... thanks, Josh. Do you mean it?"

Then I truthfully say, "Yes ... I meant every word from my heart."

That, my friend, is love.

*← what does this mean?*

You see, when you experience legalism, life becomes a bunch of "do's and don'ts" and ~~you have to~~. But when you're aware of love, life becomes about relationships and you *want to*.

Love wants to.

That being said, two people can do the exact same action or say the same words, but the motivation is what makes the difference.

*Motivation*

Either you're motivated by ...

*love* (you want to),
or
*fear* (you have to).

*← isn't it possible to be motivated by something else.*

So how do we get to this place of "want to"?

This is where grace changes everything. *Grace*

• • •

"We love because he [God] first loved us."[3]

The word *because* is extremely important. It's all a response. We don't conjure up love out of thin air. It's something we receive first.

When I say "receive" I don't mean love is held at arms length until you grab onto it. God's love is ever-present in our lives. It's always there. Or better stated, it's always *here.*

"Receiving" is when you're "awakened to" or "aware of" the fact that you are loved—not "you're not loved until you believe."

God loves us.
God loves you.
He always has.
He always will.
*Unconditionally.*

Once you allow this truth of God's love to settle in your heart, your entire world begins to change. Since your actions and mistakes don't determine God's love for you, and as you're humbled by this truth, you begin to see and love others the same way. You look past their flaws and mistakes, knowing they don't define them. And you end up loving the way God loves you.

Love somehow begins to *naturally* flow out of your life. This isn't to say you never have a choice. But in a sense, as your heart is watered with the awareness of love, your heart for others begins to *grow*. You *freely* choose to love because it's an overflow of what you're experiencing on the inside.

It no longer becomes about simply trying to follow some sort of religious principle legalistically. When your heart is *transformed* by love, you just love because that's what love does.

*Interesting questions*

Am I giving people a license to sin? Am I preaching something called "easy-believism," "greasy grace," "cheap grace," or "hyper-grace"? Am I saying that you can do whatever the hell you want because you're forgiven anyway?

Well, you actually *can* do whatever the hell you want, when you think about it. But then again, bad choices result in bad *consequences.* Those who live for *self* will eventually realize that it's not all it's cracked up to be. It's your choice.

My point is that I think many Christians are underestimating the power of love and grace. A wise person once said that whoever is forgiven much will love much.[4] I think he knew what he was talking about.

Have you wronged anyone before? I know I have.

Like every marriage, mine hasn't always been a "bed of roses." Sometimes my wife and I get into these really stupid and unnecessary arguments. Emotions often escalate and, even if I wouldn't yell, my blood would boil.

↖ *personal touch*

One time we were arguing and I thought of saying something really negative, knowing it would hurt my wife. So I bit my tongue and kept my mouth shut as best I could. Then I heard the words "Don't say it" over and over again in my mind. But, then, I ended up saying the hurtful words. *Damn it!*

Here's what's so crazy. Looking back, I realize my wife could've pointed out some of my own crap to use against me. Instead, she did something powerful.

It's not in what she said.
It's not even what she didn't say.
In fact, she didn't say anything.

Not a word.

*Benny*

Instead,
in grace, she looked into my eyes.
In grace, she gently grabbed my hand.
In grace, she looked beyond my brokenness.
And, in grace, she chose to still love me ...

*no matter what.*

Then I calmed down and began to cry.

Grace did something transformative to my soul once I became *aware* of it.

It empowered me to *put my guard down.*
It empowered me to *become more thankful.*
And it empowered me to *respond in love.*

Grace is a way to *live.* It's a way to *love* —no matter what the situation might be.

. . .

Like me, you might have moments when you'll do stupid things. You might have moments when you'll be really hard on yourself, or have your head down in shame, or have tears of regret.

But the truth may surprise you. I want you to believe that, in those moments, you can *still find yourself in God's embrace.*

Nothing you did "good" put you there. And nothing you do "bad" can take you out. You were, are, and *always* will be there—arms wrapped tightly around you—in God's embrace.

*That's grace.*

The issue is not whether we've gone too far with grace. Rather, what I'm wondering is, have we not gone far enough with it?

No one is beyond God's grace.

Absolutely no one.

FOUR

# GOSPEL: THE GOOD NEWS JUST GOT GOODER

*"If the gospel isn't good news for everybody,*
*then it isn't good news for anybody."*
**—ROB BELL**

*"When you love you should not say,*
*'God is in my heart,'*
*but rather, 'I am in the heart of God.'"*
**—KAHLIL GIBRAN**

Growing up as a Christian, I did something called door-to-door evangelism. To be honest, when I first started, it wasn't something I looked forward to. Boy, it made me nervous! It's not easy approaching random houses and trying to get every family member inside "saved" in a couple minutes.

My approach to sharing the gospel was simple:

1. Get people to believe they have a problem.
   (*"You're a sinner on the way to hell."*)

2. Offer them a solution.
   (*"Believe in Jesus and you will be saved."*)

Jesus was like a salvation ticket. Because, without him, you're screwed! But say the "sinner's prayer" in faith, then *ding, ding, ding! Jackpot!* You're on your way to heaven!

Over time I eventually became pretty confident with my approach. I wasn't afraid to share the gospel with anyone. There were some good responses, and there were also some awkward ones, not to mention the, *"Get the hell off my property!"* response.

But the negative responses didn't phase me. I wasn't surprised by them at all. In fact, "persecution" was the price I had to pay for being a "Jesus freak" who was "sold out for Christ." Rejection was something I had to get used to. After all, I was in the "business of saving souls."

. . .

I mentioned how I used to do door-to-door evangelism, but I didn't mention how *I* used to respond to it when I was on the receiving end.

Many of us know the drill.

We hear a noise coming from outside our house. We peek through the window and what do we see? A group of people—religious folks—in suits and ties getting off their bikes and walking toward our doorstep. As they get closer, we turn off the television and *shush* everyone around us. We act like we're hiding from soldiers who are about to kill us. And then we wait. We hear a couple of knocks at the door. (Dead silence.) We hold our breath. (Still dead silence.) The doorbell rings. (We start turning blue.) And then they leave. *Whew! We're safe!*

Whether they be Mormons, Evangelicals, Jehovah Witnesses, or whoever—it doesn't matter who's knocking at the door—many of us have done this magical disappearing act countless times.

But why do some of us do this? Who wouldn't want to hear good news?

• • •

Two weeks ago I went to the bank to withdraw some money from the ATM machine outside the building. Near the entrance, a kid was selling chocolates. While I was standing at the ATM, I heard a guy raising his voice. I tried minding my own business, but the guy kept yelling. It was frickin' annoying. So I looked to see what was going on. With half the guy's body sticking out of his car, and with one arm holding the door open, I realized the guy was preaching at the kid from a distance.

"You better believe in God!" he said. "He is real. Jesus is real. Believe in the Bible. Jesus is coming back soon. And those who don't believe in him will be punished."

Then the guy got into his car and drove away. (Talk about drive-by evangelism!)

I know a lot of Christians would disagree with the guy's evangelistic approach. But forget about his approach for a moment.

Isn't *that* the gospel many of us have heard? (At least a condensed version of it.)

Sure, he forgot to mention, "God loves you." And he failed to mention, "Jesus died for you." But other than that, isn't what he said the *gist* of the "good news" many of us have heard? Isn't the message basically "believe or be punished"?

Well, whether or not some Christians think so, this is what many people are hearing.

• • •

One of my first jobs as a teenager was being a tele-marketer. (FYI, if you ever want a job that destroys your self-confidence, it's this one.) My job was to sell the city's local newspaper. Did people actually need it? Well, that's debatable. But no matter what, I had to get people to believe they needed it.

Anyway, it didn't matter what time of the day I would call a random house. It was never a good time. If I called in the morning, I got, "You woke me up!" If I called in the evening, I got, "I'm so sorry, but we're eating dinner right now." And if I called any time in-between, I got, "Sorry, but we're not interested."

Ouch. "Rejection" was my middle name.

I absolutely dreaded my job. The rejections made me feel horrible—or something worse—if there is such a thing.

I remember after each rejection I'd look at the clock

and think, "Oh crap, I gotta make a hundred more of these calls before my shift is over."

I'll never forget the day this one guy picked up the phone. He "made my day." And it wasn't because I sold him a newspaper. It was actually the response he gave me after I did my little pitch.

In a typical-California-dude kind of voice he said, "Rock n' roll, man!" and hung up the phone.

That's it. But I laughed so stinkin' hard.

*Rock n' roll.* Now that sounded fun. And it sure sounded a lot better than rejection. (Actually, anything sounded better than rejection.)

Not too long after that call, I ended up leaving the job. And, no, it wasn't to become a rock star. But I knew there had to be something better for me than getting rejected everyday at work.

Sure, I could've improved my skills as a telemarketer. And some might call me "weak sauce," but, I must say, rejection can do a lot of damage to a person after awhile.

• • •

For several years I lived in the Philippines as a missionary. Now, aside from sharing the gospel at fancy churches, I was also able to minister to people at what are called the "squatter" or slum areas. These are considered the less fortunate areas of the country.

I'll never forget the time I went to an area called Smokey Mountain. Trash is stacked so high you could basically climb it. And as for the smell, don't get me started. Let's just say the guy who was with me at the time had a hard time trying to keep the previous night's dinner down.

But, come to think of it, at least he *had* dinner.

Many people who live in this area live day-to-day, picking through the landfill's rubbish for food. They have to fend for themselves and find whatever they can to survive another day.

My heart broke as I observed how some of them lived. Many of the kids I met were abandoned. They had no food to eat. They hardly had any clothes on. And many of them were getting high off glue to replace their hunger.

Behind all the dirt, the smells, and the trash, my friend and I saw beautiful people with beautiful smiles.

But what I saw didn't stop there. I started to "see" something else that day as well.

As I looked at these beautiful children, I thought, "Many of these kids can die of starvation—never hearing the gospel—especially the popular version of it widely held in North America."

You know, the ...
believe you're a sinner.
Believe Jesus is God.
Believe Jesus died on the cross for your sins.
Believe Jesus rose again on the third day.
Believe in Jesus and accept Him as your personal Lord and Savior.

Supposedly, if people do all these steps, then they get "saved" and go to heaven once they die. But if they don't ... well ... let's just say they'll be spending an eternity in another "smokey" place.

Seriously, is *that* really the gospel?

Will believing in these propositions save less fortunate souls from spending an eternity in hell?

Now, many Christians will tell you that "salvation" is ultimately based on *trusting in Jesus*—that it's all about relationship. But these same people, ironically, will also say that if you deny any of the propositions mentioned above, then you cannot be genuinely "saved."

The problem is that I wouldn't be surprised if the majority of the people living at Smokey Mountain didn't have a proper education. So, even if I did tell them to believe in X, Y, and Z in order to escape hell, would they even *understand* what I'm saying?

Because if the gospel has these requirements in order to be "saved", then here's what I'd like to do with Christians who hold to this believe-in-x-y-z-in-order-to-escape-hell-gospel so dearly.

I'd like to take them to people who are ...
in comas after a car accident,
born severely mentally retarded,
still babies,
and then I'd have them share their *believe-in-x-y-z-in-order-to-escape-hell-gospel* to these folks.[1]

I wonder how effective their message would be.

When I think about it like that, I guess the "good news" starts to sound more like "bad news" for a lot of unfortunate people around the world.

•  •  •

Back to my telemarketer story. Rejection is part of the job, isn't it? I only lasted about a week.

And I know a lot of people have had worse forms of

rejection. (Trust me, it's not the only time I've experienced rejection.)

But what about *you*?

Have you experienced rejection?

From your parents?
From the "cool" kids at school?
From the spouse who left you?

Or maybe—just maybe—you've experienced rejection from God—or at least *felt* that way because life hasn't been so kind to you.

Well, no matter where the rejection came from, how does it make you *feel*?

One day I was reading a small book by C. Baxter Kruger called *The Parable of the Dancing God*.[2] In the beginning of the book, he brings up this issue of rejection.

He asks two profound questions, which could turn a person's whole world upside-down, depending on how one answers them.

The first one is: "Have you ever met anyone who longed for rejection?"

The second one is: "Why is it that rejection hurts us so deeply?"

As for the first question, I personally never met anyone who longed for rejection. To me, that would be straight up coo-coo for anyone to long for. So the first question was an easy one for me to answer.

But the second question, *why rejection hurts us so deeply*, well, I wasn't quite sure how to answer it.

As I kept reading, Baxter gave a straightforward (yet profound) answer to the second question. It was summed up in five simple words:

*We are made for acceptance.* (Read it again and let it sink in.)

That's right. You, me, and every single person in the world are ...
made for *acceptance*.
We are made to *belong*.

You see, once we *know* we're accepted and loved, something powerful happens to us inside and out.

In other words,
*accepting our acceptance changes everything.*

• • •

Imagine going up to one of the abandoned children at Smokey Mountain and saying,

*You're an orphan.*
*You have no mom. You have no dad.*
*No one wants you. I don't even want you.*

How do you think it's going to make the child feel?

Is that love?

Now imagine going up to another abandoned child and saying,

*I love you, but ONLY IF you love me back.*
*I accept you, but ONLY IF you accept me first.*
*If you reject me, not only will I reject you, but I'll be mad at you for the rest of your life.*

(In other words, the child doesn't belong to you unless he or she does something.)

How do you think it's going to make the child feel?

Is that love?

But here's what's so interesting.

Why do so many Christians describe God this way?

For example, God says,

*I love you, but ONLY IF you love me back.*
*I accept you, but ONLY IF you accept me into your heart as your personal Lord and Savior first.*
*If you reject me, not only will I reject you, but I'll have my wrath against you for the rest of your life in a place called hell.*

(In other words, you don't belong to God unless you *do* something. God's love and acceptance end up being ... well ... conditional.)

I guess that's why the gospel was so confusing to me growing up. Although I heard that the word "love" by definition is unconditional, at the same time, I also believed God's love for me was conditional.

It's like I had to climb certain steps in order to be loved and accepted by God.

I had to *acknowledge*. (I'm getting close.)
I had to *confess*. (I'm getting closer.)
I had to *repent*. (I'm getting super close.)
I had to *believe*. (I'm there!)

Then, and only then, supposedly, I am loved and accepted by God (or "saved").

Don't get me wrong, I'm not saying acknowledging,

confessing, repenting, and believing are bad things to do. (Depends how one defines them though.) The real question is: Are those things *requirements* in order to be loved and accepted by God?

OR (and it's a big OR) ... are all those things simply *responses* of ours, knowing that, because of God's unconditional love, you, me, and every single person in the world, are already loved and accepted by him?

Big difference.

I mean, don't parents, for the most part, love their kids unconditionally no matter how much of a pain in the ass they can be at times?

Surprisingly though, when I compare God's love to that of a parent, I usually get this response from religious folks:

*Josh, God's love is different than ours. We can't understand it. We're finite. His ways are higher than our ways. His love is a mystery. Stop trying to create God in your own image.*

But seriously though, is God's love really "way out there" where we just can't understand it ... like, *at all?*

Think about it.

If God's love is so different than ours, where we just can't understand it at all, *then how would we even know what love is?*

Doesn't it say somewhere in the Bible that
God is love?[3]
And shouldn't we love others the same way
God loves us?
And aren't we also called to love our enemies?
(Sure sounds like unconditional love to me.)

So why would God expect us to love others unconditionally, yet with God, there are conditions?

Is God basically a "Do as I say but not as I do"
kind of God?

Wouldn't that make God a hypocrite?

Think about it. If God's love *is* conditional, then I guarantee you'll be spending the rest of your life trying to earn his acceptance and approval. And it'll all be based on what you do and/or believe.

You'll have no sense of security whatsoever.
Nada. Zero. Zilch.

Because you'll always be wondering, "Am I believing right? Am I acknowledging right? Confessing right?"
Am I repenting right?"

Geez, what a way to live your life.
It'll drive you nuts, I tell ya.

• • •

I love my wife. A lot. She means the world to me. (Everybody say, "Awww.") But, seriously, when we first started dating she was actually surprised by how much I loved her. All this lovey-dovey stuff was new to her. I don't blame her. I was, after all, her first boyfriend.

When we first met, she was "one tough cookie" who was very independent. She wasn't used to a guy being a gentleman towards her. She wasn't used to someone opening doors for her or paying for her food. Whenever I'd do those things, surprisingly, she'd roll her eyes in frustration. The look on her face would say, "I could've done it myself. Sheesh."[4]

But over time, the more she started to *receive* my love, the more she started to soften up. So what did I do? I kept on loving this cute and petite young woman.

And here's what's even cooler: The more she started to *believe* in my love and acceptance of her, the more she started to love and accept in return.

Did you get that?

*Her acceptance of my acceptance*
*changed our relationship completely.*

You see, when we first began our relationship, I knew that behind the tough exterior of hers, there was a gentle woman with a heart of gold. And if any of you get a chance to meet her, you'll know what I'm talking about. She is one of the sweetest persons you'll ever meet. Hands down!

Truth is, I never stopped loving her since the day we met. I always have. I always will. Other than my love deepening throughout the years, the fact that I love her never changed.

But get this: *she* changed.

She *responded* to what was *already real*
(my love and acceptance of her).

What if she never ended up believing in my love and acceptance of her? Would it make my love and acceptance any less real?

Of course not. I love and accept her whether she believes it or not.

Which brings up the question:
Is God's love and acceptance of me dependent upon me acknowledging "just right," confessing "just right,"

repenting "just right," and believing "just right"?

Hmmm ... makes you think, doesn't it?

• • •

I have a secret I want to let you in on. It's a secret that false religion doesn't want you to know. It's a secret that will mess you up forever (in a good way, of course) if you let it.

Are you ready to hear it?

The secret is this:

Right now,
at this very moment,
in spite of what you've done in the past,
before you do anything,
you,
and me,
and every single person all over the world,
are unconditionally loved,
and accepted by God.

You ... belong ... to God.

NOW.

It's not because of what you've done. And it's not even

because Jesus died on the cross.
It's because of who God is.

God is Love.
And Love, my friend, has already accepted you.

The question is: Will you accept Love?

I'm actually willing to bet my money that you already knew this "secret" too. But for sucky reasons, religion has poisoned this basic truth, which we all—deep down—already know.

But what if somebody doesn't ask Jesus into his heart? Is he or she still accepted by God?

Yes! Of course!

*That's* the GOOD NEWS!

That's why I can walk up to a random kid at Smokey Mountain, who was abandoned by everyone, including his own family, and say:

"You know what?
Everybody left you.
No one accepts you.
But guess what?
God accepts you!
I accept you!"

That is L-O-V-E.

Or would it be better to say:

"No one accepts you.
And neither does God.
Well, not until you acknowledge,
confess, repent ...
*blah, blah, blah, blah.*"

You know, the usual spiel.

No, Love sees beyond our actions—beyond our beliefs—knowing full well that they do not define us. Love looks straight into our heart.

Love sees our value.
Love sees our worth.
Love sees our true identity.

God's love for us never changes. So what happens when we *believe* in a love like this?

We change.

• • •

I remember a time in the Philippines when I was invited to speak to a group of Christians about God's love and grace. A person in the meeting seemed to be "thrown off" a bit by what I was sharing, so I asked him a couple questions in front of everyone.

"When did you get saved?" I asked.

The guy said that he "found God" at a certain age and during a certain period in his life.

"So you're saying God wasn't in your life before that?" I asked.

"How do you even think you got to that point in life of wanting to ask him into your heart unless he was already there working in you? Are you saying God was never there? And then one day you asked him into your heart, and now, all of a sudden, he's there?"

The guy was shocked by my questions. But I kept going on about how God was always in his life since day one ... *but he just didn't know it* until he awakened to the truth.

Near the end of my talk, he began to see God as much bigger, much more inclusive, and much more loving than he had ever imagined.

The truth is, before the guy "found God," God had *already* found him. Love initiated first because ... well ... that's what Love does best.

So what if the gospel is not the news where we can receive God into our lives.

*What if the gospel is the news that God has already received us into his?*[5]

Wow. You can put that in your pipe and smoke it for a while. Because for those of you who are hearing this for the very first time, that statement is going to take some time to sink in.

So let it.

You're already ...
accepted,
loved,
and in the heart of God.

Believing doesn't make this a reality. Rather, believing allows us to *experience* this reality.

• • •

For many Christians, salvation is about "dying and going to heaven." But what if salvation is much deeper than that?

What if it's more like the time my wife started to *believe* that I loved her?

What if it's more like having your *eyes opened* to the truth?

What if it's more like *waking up* to a reality, which brings newness of life?

Because once your eyes are opened to the truth of God's love and acceptance—once you wake up to its reality—how can you not be transformed?

Is this so difficult to believe?

If so, let me push it even further.
What if God is already *in* everyone?

Have you ever looked at a criminal and thought, "God is definitely *not* in that guy. He needs Jesus in his life."

But what if God is already in that criminal, and he just doesn't *know* it yet? What if God is already in the rapists, the murderers, and even the pedophiles—you know, the ones society considers to be pretty bad?[6] (You should definitely check out this endnote.)

Have you ever wondered why some unbelievers ...
appear *more loving*,
have *better marriages*,
are *better parents*,
are *more generous*,

experience *more healing,*
experience *more financial prosperity,*
than some Christians?

Truth is, whether we want to acknowledge it or not (just look around for goodness sake), the light shines everywhere. Open your eyes. The only time you'll ever see darkness is when you *close your eyes* to the truth, believe the lies, and reject love.

The late Mother Teresa recounted a story where a man approached her and said, "I am an atheist." But, according to her, this atheist spoke so beautifully about love.

Her response to him was, "You cannot be an atheist if you speak so beautifully about love. Where there is love, there is God. God is love."[7]

*Where there is love, there is God.*

Beautiful.

• • •

I'll never forget the story[8] I heard evangelical author Tony Campolo share during an interview he had with Charlie Rose. According to Campolo, his Baptist missionary friend went to China and met a Buddhist monk. The missionary friend opened up his Bible and explained the things of Jesus to this monk. And as the story of Jesus was being told, the monk started to weep.

"Will you accept Jesus as your Savior?" the missionary asked.

"Accept him?" the monk said. "I have always known this Jesus. You have given me his name. You have told me what he has done on the cross. You talked about the resurrection. But even as you were speaking, his Spirit within me was saying, as you read from the book, 'He's speaking of me. He's speaking of me.'"

Wow.

Folks, God is alive and well in many places and in many people that we can't even imagine. Maybe Christ is much more cosmic than we'd like to think.

I want to end this chapter with one of my favorite parts from the book *The Shack*. In it, there's a conversation where the protagonist asks Jesus if *all roads lead to him.*

To his question, Jesus replies, "Not at all. ... Most roads don't lead anywhere. What it does mean is that I will travel any road to find you."[9]

Any road.

That sounds like the kind of love I believe in.

God is not far from anybody.

So if God loves and accepts all of humanity,
Then my question is:

Why can't we?

FIVE

# THE CROSS:
# THE SCHIZOPHRENIC GOD

*"I have described atonement, the central doctrine
of Christianity, as vicious, sado-masochistic and repellent. ...
If God wanted to forgive our sins, why not just forgive them,
without having himself tortured and executed in payment?"*
**—RICHARD DAWKINS**

*"But I have seen his face and heard his voice in the face and
the voice of Jesus Christ; and I say this is our God."*
**—GEORGE MACDONALD**

There is a scene in the film *The Life of Pi* where the main character, Pi, tells his story of how he met Christ in the mountains when he was twelve years old. As the story goes, he goes into a church on a dare to drink the holy water. Once he completes the dare, he looks around the sanctuary and looks perplexed while staring at the various images of Jesus being crucified. He is then surprised by a priest who offers him a glass of water.

After taking a sip from the glass, Pi looks up and points to an image of a suffering Jesus being crucified:

*Pi*: Why would a God do that? Why would he send his own son to suffer for the sins of ordinary people?

*Priest*: Because he loves us. God made himself approachable to us, human, so we could understand him. We can't understand God in all his perfection, but we can understand God's son and his suffering as we would of brother's.

Then the scene fast-forwards to the adult version of Pi as he recalls the story.

*Pi* (shaking his head): That made no sense. Sacrificing the innocent to atone for the sins of the guilty. What kind of love is that?

• • •

We've all heard it before, haven't we?

"Jesus died on the cross for you."
"Jesus paid your debt."
"Jesus paid it all."

But what does it all mean?

For years, the whole "Jesus paid your debt" thing made sense to me.

Until ... well ... it didn't.

The cross is central to Christianity. It is central to the gospel. You can see crosses everywhere—around people's necks, tattooed on people's bodies, and even on top of church buildings.

So what exactly happened at the cross? And why did Jesus die?

Well, let me tell you what I was taught:

We all sinned by breaking God's Law
(the Ten Commandments).
We all became guilty before God.
And because God is "holy" (in a legal sense),
he won't allow sin to go unpunished.
Because justice requires *punishment*.
And God's wrath must be *satisfied*.

But,
because the Father loves us,
he sent his son, Jesus
(who offered himself willingly),
to suffer for us.
On the cross,
the guilt of the entire human race,
and all of God's wrath,
was placed upon Jesus.

In short, Jesus, God's innocent son, was punished "for" and "instead" of us in order to manifest God's love and holiness.

Traditionally, this has been called *penal substitutionary atonement theory*.[1] (Such an awkward name.) Some popular theologians have even gone so far as to say that this is the gospel. I even heard a well-known pastor during an interview say that if you reject this version of the gospel, then you can't be a Christian. (Those are pretty strong statements, don't you think?)

Well, whether or not you've even heard of the name "penal substitution," it doesn't matter. I think the majority of the Christian world is at least familiar with it in theory.

To give an illustration of this version of the gospel, it's very much like a courtroom setting.

Notice the language.

There's a judge (God).
You broke a law (the Ten Commandments)
and are therefore guilty.
You incurred a debt you cannot pay.
But someone (Jesus) comes along and pays the debt
for you.

Come to think of it, this gospel seems rather devoid
of relationship if you ask me. It sounds more like a
"legal" and impersonal gospel if anything.

• • •

I remember my hardcore evangelistic days when I
used to go around making people feel like crap when
I'd share my faith with them. My method: Tell them
the bad news first ("You're a sinner who broke God's
commandments") before I told them the good news
("Jesus was punished for you").

Surprisingly, my little "gospel spiel" worked with some
people. But, obviously, not with others. It didn't make
sense to them. And I didn't know why, because it
made complete sense to me. I held onto this version
of the gospel for years.

It was the only gospel I knew.

Once I reached my thirties, I was still traveling and preaching this gospel.

"Jesus paid it all!" I'd say, and "amens" would be heard throughout the crowds.

"You'll never be punished, because Jesus was punished for you!" I'd continue. Once again, more "amens."

I'd keep going. "And ALL of God's WRATH was poured out on his son." Then looks of astonishment would be on people's faces. They were amazed by how good God was.

*Err ... hold up ... wait a minute! People were blessed to hear that God the Father unleashed his anger on his innocent Son?*

In a word, yes.

But over time ... something happened to me. I'll never forget the feeling. In it's initial stages, it was a sense of awkwardness. I reached a point where I'd be preaching about God's love and grace at different religious events and feel very uncomfortable saying *that* last statement—you know, the one about "God's wrath being poured out on his son."

For instance, I spoke at a church and was getting ready to say *that* statement. It was sort of like a climax to my message. Then right when I was about to say it, I hesitated.

Then I spoke at another church and the same thing happened. I got ready to say it, but I hesitated. And, this time, I couldn't say *that* statement.

Then it happened at another church. And another church. You get the point. I was honestly wondering what the heck was going on. Why couldn't I say *that* statement anymore?

I didn't read a book telling me it was wrong. I didn't hear a preacher say it was wrong.

To be honest, it just *felt wrong.*

There I was at all these religious meetings ... talking about God's unconditional love, his amazing grace, when all of a sudden, in the same breath, I'd start talking about God punishing and unleashing all his wrath on his own innocent son.

*Talk about a schizophrenic God!*

You see, when it comes to salvation, I was taught to ask the question: What are we are saved from?

Growing up, the answers were basically two things: "sin" and "hell."

I remember back during my college days, one of my favorite theologians at the time said something on the radio I'll never forget.

He said it's ultimately not a matter of *what* we're saved from, but *who* we're saved from.

In sum, he said: When it comes to salvation, we're ultimately saved from ... *God.*

*Saved from God?!* Yup, that's what I heard.

To be more specific, he explained in more detail that we are saved from "God's wrath."

And that's what I uncritically accepted as an answer at the time and "believed" for years.

But in recent years, thankfully, I finally questioned that idea and thought to myself, "If Jesus saved us from God (the Father), then what *kind* of God is that?"

The "good news" started to sound more like the "disturbing news."

• • •

The way we view the cross, I believe, says a lot about how we view God. I also believe the way we view God ultimately shapes the way we live our lives.

Check this out. The gospel today presents a kind of God who is basically saying this:

*I'm extremely angry with you because of sin (even if it's a "white lie").*
*And because I'm holy, somebody needs to "pay the price" (aka: suffer).*
*But because I love you so much,*
*I'm going to violently kill my own innocent son.*
*Once I do, then I won't be angry with you anymore.*

Of course, you won't find Christians saying it in exactly these words. They'll usually soften it up and add the fact that God desires a personal relationship. And they probably won't use the words "violently kill" either. But the theology and mechanics of how the cross brings about salvation, according to this version of the gospel, is exactly the way I described it above.

You know what?

It ... just ... doesn't ... make ... sense ... anymore.

This gospel makes God seem like those people with anger-management issues who, when they're mad, have to hit something. Anything. It could be a wall, a punching bag, a pillow, whatever. Like them, God is so pissed-off he needs to hit something or someone. Anyone.[2]

Luckily (for us at least), his son Jesus (the unlucky one) says, "You can hit me, Father." So what does the Father do? He violently bruises and crushes[3] his innocent son in order to satisfy his anger.

Now, doesn't that sound like some sort of *cosmic child abuse?*[4]

One time I had a Bible study with a group of people where we were discussing this very topic. I told them I was beginning to question this version of the gospel. A girl I never met seemed offended the moment I brought up the challenge and was quick to defend this version.

"Jesus' death," she said, "was like a sacrifice. It's like someone taking a bullet for you."

"OK," I responded, "but guess who pulled the trigger? The *Father.*"

For some strange reason though, she seemed offended even more by my response. I didn't understand why. Because according to her illustration that's exactly what's going on.

According to those who believe this version
of the gospel,
God killed his own innocent son,
so he wouldn't have to kill you and me.

(Any loving parents out there?)

Punishing the innocent in place of the guilty? I seriously don't understand how anyone can justify this kind of logic. In fact, I believe it defies logic of any kind.

• • •

Now, if you believe in something called the Trinity where the Father, Son, and Holy Spirit are equal and one in unity, then this version of the gospel definitely messes up the godhead for you.

For instance, the way it all plays out is there's an extremely angry side of God (the Father) who is un-forgiving towards you because of sin. In fact, he can't even look at you because he's so holy. Then there's this other side of God (Jesus) who is gracious and forgiving towards you in spite of your sin. In fact, he even "becomes sin" (whatever that means).

What the?! So God ends up being both the problem and the solution? Yup. And get this ... it all happens within himself (or themselves).

No matter how strange it sounds, Jesus helps the Father to *like* us. I know, it sounds weird. That's be-cause it is. Jesus is like the middle-man who keeps the Father from "beating the snot" out of humanity. It's as if the Father hates us so much because of sin, but once we place our faith in Jesus, then *BAM!*, God magically no longer sees "us" in our sin anymore. Instead, he sees his perfect Son. It's like we wear a "Jesus costume" which deceives the Father and keeps him from hurting the ones wearing the costume.

But if that's the case, where's the *unity* among the Trinity? It's hard to imagine one member of the Trinity (the Father) punishing another member of the Trinity (Jesus)—not to mention an innocent one.

Sounds like *divine domestic violence* to me.

I don't think God's justice was ever meant to be purely *retributive*,
rather, I believe, it was (and still is) *restorative*.[5]

Imagine your child does something that pisses you off and you decide to punish him. But right before you spank him, his brother gets in the way and says, "Hit me, Mom (or Dad). I know I didn't do anything wrong. But go ahead. Let all your anger out on me, so you'll be satisfied."

Justice?

Nah, you'd probably think the brother is crazy.

• • •

Oh, and another thing, according to this gospel, God can't simply forgive sin. He needs to be compensated. He withholds forgiveness until someone worthy enough will "pay up." It's an economy of exchange. Tit for tat. Forgiveness, for God, has to do with balancing the scales.

But here's the problem. Let's say you owe me money. And let's say I'm so furious I won't let you "off the hook." But the sad thing is, you can't pay me. Fortunately for you, someone comes along and pays the debt *you* owe me. Then I look at *you* and say,
*"OK, I totally forgive you now."*

Think about it. How is that even forgiveness? I got my stinkin' money!

Let me tell you what *real* forgiveness looks like. It's when you owe me money, and with compassion, I look at you and say, "I release you from your debt."

*That's forgiveness.*

Forgiveness is about setting the guilty person free. Because if God needed someone to pay a debt, and the debt was actually paid, then there's actually *nothing* left to forgive.

Forgiveness, by definition, cannot be a payment.[6]

I mean, if God truly forgives, then why any punishment at all? Forgiveness is forgiveness. If anyone *is* punished, whether innocent or guilty, then the word "forgiveness" simply loses its meaning completely.

To make things even more complicated, this version of the gospel also contradicts the life and teachings of Jesus himself. Jesus, from what I'm aware of, revealed the heart of God. His gospel is more of a "turn the other cheek" kind of gospel.

But this "penal" version of the gospel is more of an "eye for an eye" kind of gospel. It's not real forgiveness. It's not real grace.

Jesus didn't turn to those who screwed up and say, "Hey, before I forgive you, somebody needs to be punished. Anybody. It doesn't even have to be you. For crying out loud, it can even be someone innocent. Any takers? I just need to unleash my wrath!" No, that's silly. Of course Jesus didn't say that.

Check this out: Jesus *freely* forgave people.

Why? Because that's his heart. He understood that real forgiveness doesn't *depend* on a person's "repentance" (change of mind). Instead, once it's received in humility, forgiveness can *lead* to it.

• • •

Also, I often hear Christians talk about how Jesus had to die and be *punished* by God the Father. I even hear preachers say, "Jesus was born to die."

Is that true? Was Jesus' *main goal* to die? Really?

If so, then why didn't God punish and kill baby Jesus while he was still in the manger? What took God so darn long to do what he needed to do? Why the thirty-three years delay?

Or, on the other hand, if Jesus' goal was to die in order satisfy his Father's wrath, then why couldn't Jesus simply die of *old age*? Why couldn't *natural death* satisfy the Father? Death is death, right?

I mean, it's not like God the Father had to wait for Jesus to sin and be guilty. Jesus died, according to many Christians, an innocent man, remember?

Think about it. If God orchestrated Jesus' suffering, and it was all part of his divine plan, then why did he feel the need to use violent people to accomplish his purpose? Why did he have to do it in such a cruel and horrific way?

Floggings.
Beatings.
Torturing.
Mocking.

Dude, that's *barbaric*.

Not to mention, this was all for the public eye to see. Does God like shaming people in front of others? Does he get a kick out of it?

For him to suffer such things for God's justice and anger to be satisfied, well, I wouldn't even wish those horrible things on my worst enemies.

Not only that, Christians say that *you* and *me*, people who exist 2,000 years after the actual crucifixion, put Jesus on the cross.

But what did *I* do that would make Jesus deserve such a beating through the providential guidance of God the Father? What if, hypothetically, the worst thing I ever did was steal? Would Jesus still deserve to be punished the way he was? He was beaten to a pulp. C'mon, even if I was a serial killer, I still wouldn't think Jesus deserved to suffer such excruciating pain on my behalf.

What he suffered was a *living hell* on earth. In fact, Christians go even further and say he literally suffered our *hell*, so we wouldn't have to "go to hell" when we die.

But if it's true that Jesus suffered our *hell* on the cross, so we wouldn't have to go there when we die—and if hell is *eternal* (as many people claim)—then why was Jesus on the cross for only several hours?

Why not forever?

Sure, people can say it's because Jesus is God, so it's different somehow. But, still, that doesn't adequately answer the question for me. If he has to suffer *everything* I will suffer if I reject him, then his suffering should have lasted forever, right?

Am I missing something?

• • •

As I already mentioned, our view of the cross impacts the way we view God. So it really all comes down to what we "see."

For me, what I see happening on that rugged cross 2,000 years ago was a revelation of God's unconditional love and not a demonstration of his wrath (the pissed-off kind) being poured out on his innocent son.

If God is love, then love doesn't hold grudges.

So through the eyes of love, let me tell you what I *do* and *don't* see happening on the cross.

I don't see a God who demands a sacrifice.
I see a God who, in Christ, becomes a sacrifice.

I don't see a God who kills an innocent victim.
I see a God who, in Christ, becomes the victim.

I don't see a God who is violent and retributive.
I see a God who, in Christ, is nonviolent and
restorative.

I don't see a God whose wrath needs
to be appeased.
I see a God who, in Christ, appeases
the wrath of humanity.

I don't see a God who is thirsty for blood
because of sin.
I see a God who, in Christ, sheds his blood
and forgives sin.

I see a God who, in Christ, subjects himself to
the collective violence of an entire community.[7]

I see a God who, in Christ, reveals the true nature of
violence to its full extent—understanding that violence
never ultimately solves violence.

I see a God who, in Christ, believes that only self-
sacrificial love brings about true justice and peace.

I see a God who, in Christ,
*loves* his enemies
and *subverts* the "wisdom of the world" (violence)
to show us a better way (peace and non-violence).

I see a God who, in Christ,
shows us the path he is willing to take ...
to show us how much he loves the world.

*No matter what the cost.*

SIX

# HELL:
# TOO HOT TO HANDLE

*"Abandon all hope upon entering here!"*
**—DANTE'S INFERNO**

*"Christianity supplies a Hell for the people who disagree with you and a Heaven for your friends."*
**—ELBERT HUBBARD**

I want you to imagine with me for a moment.

Imagine someone you *dearly* love right now. Not just anyone. But someone who means the world to you. It can be your spouse or even your own child. Let it be someone so important to you that just thinking about this person makes you feel so much love. Let it be someone you can't imagine living without.

In fact, let it be someone you'd even sacrifice your life for.

But, for the sake of this thought experiment, let's say this person isn't a Christian—at least not in any traditional sense. And let's say this person knows the ABC's of the Christian religion and has even done the whole "church thing" for several years.

But, the *brand of Christianity* he or she was taught doesn't make any sense to this person. And the *version of God* this person inherited throughout the years from friends and family just … well, doesn't make any sense to him or her either. And to make matters worse, the hypocrisy found among many Christians has been another obstacle, which keeps him or her from converting to Christianity.

But, this person, the one you dearly love,
*still loves people.*

This person has questions about God and is even open—searching for answers—but simply hasn't "arrived" just yet when it comes to embracing religious faith.

But, this person, the one you dearly love,
*still loves you.*

Then one day, unexpectedly, this person gets into a car accident and is pronounced dead on arrival.

This person, *the one you dearly love*,
didn't die a Christian.

So ... the BIG QUESTION: Where is this person *now*?

Well, according to many fundamentalist Christians, this person is in ... yup, that's right,

*HELL.*

And for how long will this person be in *HELL*?

A hundred years? Nope.
A thousand years? Nope.
A million years? Nope.
What about a trillion years? Not even close.

*Forever.*

Sadly, there's no escape because, according to many fundamentalist Christians, hell is ...
*eternal* ...
*conscious* ...
*torment.*

Try letting those three words sink in for a bit before moving on to the next paragraph.

• • •

You see, stories like the one I just mentioned happen everyday. Even if it was a thought experiment, it's a reality for many people who lose their loved ones un- expectedly, which makes it such an important subject to address. I'm sure many are left wondering where their dead loved ones "go" when they "transition" to the "other side." I know I would.

I seriously believe religion has screwed up a lot of people by using fear. Religion says that unless you cross your *t's* or dot your *i's* just right (by believing in the right religion), then an eternal torture chamber awaits you.

I don't know any doctrine more extreme and disturb- ing than this one, to be quite honest.

Can you imagine a child hearing about hell for the very first time and wondering if he or she will be able to avoid it? It's torture. What kind of loving parent would want to instill such an unnecessary fear into an innocent child?

• • •

I finally found the courage to start questioning hell several years ago. For years, prior to me questioning, hell was my default answer whenever someone would ask me where non-Christians went when they died. For me, it was a given: *All non-Christians go to hell.* Period. It was something I thought the Bible said. Why? Because that's what religion taught me.

For most of my life,
I believed people deserved to go to hell because they didn't believe in God ... *the way I did.*

I remember the days when I'd be in a public place. I'd look around at the people's faces around me and think, "Man, most of these people, if they were to die tonight, will be spending an eternity in hell."

Those moments seriously made me sad. I mean, if you *really* think about it, how could it not? I'm not frickin' heartless.

But I wasn't going to take things sitting down. I wasn't going to "let the devil have his way." So I committed myself to "evangelizing" the lost wherever I went. I didn't want anyone's "blood on my hands." I didn't want to be in heaven one day "looking down" at all those unfortunate souls in hell and have them "look up" and say to me, "If only *you* shared with me! Why didn't you share?!"

I didn't want to have a guilt trip in heaven—if that's even possible.

I must admit, trying to "save" as many people as possible before I died was a huge responsibility for me. But it was one I was willing to carry.

For years, almost every week, I shared my faith with unbelievers. A lot of them. But of all the countless people I evangelized and helped lead in the "sinner's prayer," it still wasn't enough. Those I led to Christ, in my small part of the world, still couldn't compare to the hundreds of thousands of people all around the world who die everyday not converting to Christianity and who, ultimately, end up spending an eternity "apart from God."

The burden seemed too much for me to handle. *Why did God have to make this way of "saving" the world so difficult?* It seemed unrealistic.

But my thoughts began to change when I finally was willing to question this very "sacred" doctrine called *hell*. I was finally open to the possibility that it might not be true. This was a huge step for me, because I never thought I'd have the guts to even question it. Seriously, it made me uncomfortable. (In fact, it might even make you uncomfortable. So I admire you if you keep on reading.)

But I knew it was the next step in my faith journey.

You see, what got me to finally question the doctrine of hell wasn't because of any book. And it wasn't because any of my favorite theologians rejected it either.

Honestly, the real questioning began once I started to understand *love* better. (I'm dead serious.)

I couldn't reconcile *eternal conscious torment* with *God's unconditional love.* How the hell could those six words go together?

As I continued to grow in my understanding of love (as I still do), my perspective of everything began to change.

Love changed the way I ...
viewed God,
understood the gospel,
related with people,
and saw *life*.

Once I began to see everything through the lens of love, I started to realize how the popular evangelical gospel is, in essence, a "turn or burn" gospel—a "believe or else" sort of message.

And, finally, I sensed the urgency to say something about it.

• • •

I've attended religious meetings where the preacher would talk about God's love the majority of the message, but toward the end of it, he'd ask, "Do you know where you'll end up if you die tonight? If not, believe in Jesus and you will go to heaven. But if you reject him, you will be separated from him forever in hell."

Now, I don't know about you, but when I hear messages like this, I think it reduces Jesus to being two things:

*Fire insurance.*
*And a salvation ticket.*

It's *like* the preacher is saying,
"God loves you sooooooooooooo much! But, hey, if you don't like him back, well, then he created a very special place for you to suffer."

He continues, "But there's a way to avoid this place. Jesus is your ticket who will help you escape the flames of hell."

OK, a preacher doesn't usually put it in those exact words, but it is pretty much what people are *hearing*.

Come to think of it, with that kind of threat, who wouldn't "love" God back? *Give me the Jesus ticket!*

•  •  •

What's even crazier is this:

If an eternal hell does exist, then God must be the one sustaining it. I've heard people say "hell is the *absence* of God." Well, I'm not so sure about that, because if you believe God is *everywhere*, then he must be in hell, too. After all, hell cannot exist on its own, right? It's not self-existent.

So if hell does exist, can you imagine a good God allowing and sustaining the suffering of those he loves forever? (I know, it's hard for me to imagine a good God doing such a thing, too.)

Some die-hard-hell-believers will say, "Josh, just because you can't imagine it, doesn't mean it's not real. What does the Bible have to say about it?"

Well, if we're going to be honest readers of the Bible, then we have to acknowledge the fact that the Bible actually says a lot of different things about the subject of hell. In fact, sometimes even contradictory things. But I'm not trying to "get all academic" here. This book isn't meant for that. Which is why I encourage you to do your own homework and not just take my word for it.[1]

Look up the words "hell," "eternal," "everlasting," and "wrath" in their original language and you'll be surprised with what you'll find. I can get technical here and break it all down for you, but then you'd still be taking my word for it. Do yourself a favor and find out for yourself. Don't always leave your "beliefs" in the hands of the theologians—especially when it comes to important doctrines such as this one.

You see, what the average religious person doesn't realize is that we have a lot of Bible translations, which differ significantly with one another. Some Bible translations contain the word "hell" numerous times, while other translations contain the word "hell" only a few times. But check this out (and this is where it gets even more interesting): *Some Bible translations don't contain the word "hell" at all.*

Hmmm ...
As you dig deeper into your studies, what you'll discover is that the Greek and Hebrew words we use for

"hell" in our English Bible mean totally different things from what we've been taught. *How crazy is that?!*

What's also interesting, ironically, is once you look into the passages which supposedly refer to the afterlife, you'll be able to find support for several contradictory positions concerning the doctrine of hell.

What I mean is, depending on the Bible translation, you'll find verses supporting an *everlasting* hell; you'll find verses supporting unbelievers being *annihilated*; and you'll even find verses supporting a *temporary* hell.

So which is it? It can be so "damning" ... I mean, so damn confusing, which is why this is such a hotly debated topic. (And, yes, pun intended.)

• • •

I personally believe the doctrine of hell creates more questions than answers—which is why I have found many explanations from Christians throughout the years to be less than satisfying.

I mean,
why would God, being all-knowing, create people he already knows ahead of time would reject him?
In response to this question, I've heard several eternal-

hell-defenders say, "Well, it's better for God to have loved and lost than never to have loved at all."

Sure, that's a nice little quote, but how is it really "better to have loved and lost than never to have loved at all" when it comes to the idea of hell?

Let's say, for instance, before you become a parent, you have knowledge of the future. And let's say you know ahead of time that the potential child you and your partner can create will *definitely* go to hell once he or she dies. Would you go through with it? Would it really be worth loving your child for maybe a little over seventy or eighty years at the expense of your child burning in a torture chamber for all eternity? Wouldn't it have been better to save your child from an eternal torture chamber by not letting him or her be born in the first place?

• • •

I've also heard Christians say that eternal hell is well deserved because, although we commit finite sins, they're committed against an *infinite* God.

But still, how does that make any sense? We don't even do that in our society today. Aren't people punished based on the *severity* of the crime and not necessarily who their crime is committed against?[2]

Is it really fair for someone to be *infinitely* punished for *finite* sins? Shouldn't the "punishment fit the crime"?

I mean, even for the worst "sin" you can think of, would the infinite punishing of someone really balance things out? I cannot fathom the idea of how a good God can allow people to be tortured in an eternal hell for sins committed over a course of what—probably less than ninety years? The idea of it all seems so crazy to me.

. . .

Also, how is it *just* for a God to hold someone accountable for a gospel they've never even heard? We need to be realistic here. Many people throughout the world—especially those who live in the "boonies"—have never heard this gospel message. So do those people burn forever because they were born in the wrong place, at the wrong time, and in the wrong religion?

I've heard some Christians say that those who never hear the gospel are not held responsible. In other words, if they don't know the truth, then they are no longer responsible for what they "don't know"—and therefore won't go to hell.

If that's the case, then why tell them the gospel and make them "responsible"? Why put them at risk? Isn't

it better for them
years with an ab
way to a heaven

Wouldn't that be
a bad decision (r
on earth instead
an eternity in he

. . .

Is there a time limit to God's love? Is it like this: When you're alive on earth (and for some, it's very short) God is constantly wooing you with love, but once you die, then *BAM!* it's a different story? *It's time to suffer wrath!* Does God's loving pursuit towards humanity end at death?

But I always heard "love is patient."

Sure, people can say that God was patient with people during their time on earth, but like I already mentioned, many have experienced very short lives.

. . .

Do people who reject "fundamental" doctrines like the deity of Christ, the resurrection, and the Trinity really deserve an eternal hell?

I've heard Christians say, "It's about relationship, not religion." But I've also heard the same people say that if you reject the "fundamental" doctrines I just mentioned, then you're not a Christian—which means you're not saved—which means ... well ... you're not going to heaven.

The problem is that I've met numerous Christians who have no idea how to even articulately explain (let alone understand) the doctrines mentioned above. What about those who are uneducated or those raised in less fortunate areas? How much doctrine can they fully grasp before making a "fully informed decision"?

I've even met "mature" Christians who've reached periods in their lives where they got confused and began questioning their faith. They still believed in God, but they weren't sure what else to believe because their "secular" university messed them up intellectually. And I've certainly had my own moments of doubts concerning certain doctrines. (As you can see in this book.)

So should those of us who have doubts, or moments of unbelief, and who die during these periods, remain apart from God forever simply because we couldn't grasp all this doctrine stuff? Do people go to hell simply because they're confused with what to believe? Is God really that cold-hearted?

• • •

I've heard defenders of eternal hell say, "God sends nobody to hell. God gave people free will. So people send themselves there." I once heard a Christian even go so far as to say that those in hell *want* to be there. (I seriously wonder what that person was smoking when he said that.)

I mean, if the descriptions of hell I heard growing up from Christians are true—you know—things like being tortured by demons day and night, being burned in flames, and having no access to water—then who in the world would want to be in that kind of environment? I know I wouldn't.

Because if it is true that people used their free will to *get into* hell, then my question is: Why can't they use their free will to *get out* of hell? Are people no longer free once they die? Isn't freedom the thing God has given us because love gives room for choice?

And even if people can resist God with their will, can God's love be resisted *forever*? Why do people have to remain stuck in hell? Can't they learn their lesson in hell and eventually turn to God? Why does death have to be final?[3]

• • •

When I lived in the Philippines I attended a Bible study where a good friend of mine talked about God being a "God of hope." It was a beautiful message. In fact, I couldn't agree with him more. But a question came to mind during the meeting, which I ended up asking him afterward.

"Would God ever create a situation for a person," I asked,
"where there is absolutely no hope whatsoever?"[4]
"No," he said.
"Then what about hell?" I asked.

Then we both looked at each other as if we could read each other's minds. It was questions like this which helped the both of us start digging deeper into this topic. We both desired to see a consistency in God's loving and gracious character before and after people die, because there's no consistency in the traditional view of hell.

• • •

You see, if I had a son, no matter how bad his behavior might be, I would never think he'd deserve an eternal hell. That thought wouldn't even cross my mind.[5] Because no matter what, he would always be my son.

And even if it were possible for him to make bad

choices, which would "send" him to hell ... well ... because of my unconditional love for him, *I would go into hell myself and save him.*

Would I give up on him? Hell no! No loving parent would give up on his or her child. So why would God do any less for us?

Because for me, to be honest, I'd have a hard time worshiping a God who'd do anything less than what any decent human being would do.

Not only would that make God look bad, in my opinion, but how would that even be a good "biblical" story? Think about the story many of us have been told. It sounds much different once it's all laid out for us to see:

God creates billions of people through Adam and Eve.

*All of humanity* is affected by Adam's sin and are on their way to hell.

But God, because he's so smart and loving, has a plan.

God sends his unique son to "potentially" save the world.

But, only a *few* people believe.

And, therefore, the majority of humanity will spend the rest of their lives "separated" from God's love and presence in a place called hell.

*Forever.*

The end. (Actually, there is no "end" for those suffering forever, right?)

If that's the "big picture" of the Bible story, then isn't it a pretty crappy ending? Couldn't God have come up with a better story? I mean, losing the majority of his children because of sin, free will, or the devil, well, that's a bummer, ain't it? It kind of makes you question the whole purpose of it all. Why would God even bother creating and enjoying his creation for a finite period of time when the majority of his children will be "separated" from him forever?

• • •

And another thing. If religious folks *really* believe the majority of people on planet earth are on their way to an eternal torture chamber, then shouldn't they be outside preaching the gospel 24/7? Shouldn't they drop everything at this very moment and abandon their cozy lives to lead every single person they meet to Christ? Did they forget that countless people die every day without ever hearing the gospel or converting to Christianity?

It's just a thought.

Or maybe these religious folks really don't believe in an eternal hell.
Or maybe, although it may be hard to admit, they're just lazy.

But who knows?

• • •

Then there are those who bring up the "not-so-lovable ones." Sure, there are a lot of "evil"[6] people out there who have done a lot of horrible things. I'm not here to point fingers, because we're all potentially "evil" people (not by nature but behavior). There are people like murderers, rapists, and dictators who—when we're feeling angry—we believe should "rot in hell" forever. It's understandable. When someone has hurt you or someone you love, it's almost our natural instinct to wish the worst on him or her.

People like Hitler, Stalin, Osama Bin Laden, and Kim Jong-il seem to be, for many people, the perfect candidates for an eternal hell. They supposedly "deserve" eternal damnation.

Maybe. But here's what I'm wondering.

What about the *millions* of victims who suffered a "living hell" at the hands of these "hell-deservers"?

Think about it. Many of these victims were beaten, tortured, treated like dogs, and murdered. I can take a wild guess that many of them weren't even "born-again" evangelical Christians.

So where are they now?

That's right. According to many fundamentalist Christians, they're right there in hell—*still burning*—right along with their persecutors. Why?

Because they didn't convert to Christianity during their time on earth.[7]

And while we're at it, why don't we throw Mother Teresa in hell as well? After all, according to some Protestants, she wasn't a genuine believer, because she was Roman Catholic and lived by "works" rather than faith. So she, along with Hitler and company, are suffering torture for all eternity ... *together*.

But let's say, for the sake of argument, that one of these "evil" dictators—who have killed millions of innocent people by the way—said the "sinner's prayer" and believed right before he died.

Where would he have gone—at least according to evangelical Christians?

That's right. Heaven!

Really?
Is that how things work in this life? I'm not saying I understand it all, don't get me wrong. I'm simply questioning if things are really this black and white.

• • •

Please don't misunderstand me. I'm not saying "sin" doesn't have to be dealt with. And neither am I saying those who screw up (which is all of us) can never receive grace. But this whole "who's in and who's out" based on what you do or how you believe seems questionable to me.

But let's get back to the whole "punishment" deal.

Let's say a guy went on a killing spree and gets locked up behind bars for twenty years. Then what? How does that ultimately solve anything?

Isn't the problem much *deeper*?

Sure, a dangerous person is off the streets for a certain period of time. But what happens once he gets out? What if he goes on a killing spree again? Thing is, he can end up being the same person he was when he first got locked up—or possibly even worse.

Someone can say, "Well, if he doesn't change, then that's why we keep him locked up for life." (Which is how eternal hell can be justified.)

Sure, that solves the problem of others getting attacked by him. Thing is, that doesn't solve the problem of *him—the individual.* Isn't the criminal, aside from how others may see him, God's precious creation? Isn't he still made in the image of God?

Isn't he someone's son?
Couldn't he be someone's father?
Or even someone's brother?

Would any of you parents ever give up on your rebellious child no matter how "bad" he or she is?

And what if, during the time the criminal was behind bars, there was a positive change in him? What if the man repented (changed his mind), found forgiveness, and had a change of heart? Wouldn't that make all the difference in the world? Wouldn't that be the hope of his parents, or his child, or even his siblings?

I guess that's what it all comes down to, doesn't it?

Is God a God of *retribution*?

Or is God a God of *restoration*?[8]

Instead of letting our view of eternal hell shape our understanding of God, what if we let our view of God shape our view of hell?

Is a loving God more concerned about "giving people what they deserve"? Or is he, like any other loving father, more concerned about his child being restored?

For instance, would I discipline my son if he screws up? Sure. Because that's what loving fathers do, right? To me, justice isn't saying, "Everything you did was OK. Do whatever you want, because there are no consequences." No, my heart for my child would be to see him eventually restored back into relationship with me and those he hurt. I would want him to experience *forgiveness*, *grace*, and *unconditional love*, because those are the very things, which I believe, *genuinely* transform the human heart.

Not guilt.
Not punishment.
Not shame.

Those three things never bring about a genuine transformation of the human heart.
Love is what heals pain.

Hurt people hurt people, right? We all do stupid things when we're hurting. So why can't God be more understanding? Why can't God take all our pain and bring healing (no matter how long it takes) rather than unending punishment?

Why can't *that* be true justice?

Because if hell is unending punishment, then evil is not defeated and overcome by love. Rather, evil becomes the victor. And eternal hell keeps the cycle of evil in motion forever. It keeps evil demons doing evil things to evil people. There's nothing ultimately redemptive in that.

So does evil win over God's love?
Is that the end of the story?

Is that true justice?

• • •

I've had people say to me, "Josh, it doesn't matter how you feel about hell. And it doesn't have to make any sense to you either."

It's responses like this where religion has gotten people to somehow detach themselves from love and common sense.

Let me get this straight. People (including those I love) are being tortured day and night for all eternity and "it doesn't matter how I feel"?

Have we become heartless people?
Have we abandoned our natural senses?
Have we forgotten to read the Bible with our hearts?

I've heard people say, "Well, *I* would never let people burn in hell forever. But I'm not God. God is God. And he can do whatever he wants."

But think about it.
*Why* wouldn't *you* let people burn in hell forever?

Here's my guess.
I think it's because you know ... and I know ... that letting people burn in hell for all eternity is not love!

Love never gives people no hope.
Love, being unfailing, restores.
Love never gives up.

• • •

I'll never forget the time I first opened up to my parents concerning my thoughts on hell. Sure enough, it caught them off guard. They were surprised to hear their own son, who was a pastor and missionary, was questioning this "essential" doctrine.

During our three-hour conversation, I asked my dad where Grandma was, since she passed away a long time ago. He said he knew she was in heaven, because he "led her to Christ" right before she died. So because of his witness, he felt assured of his mother's final destination.

Then I asked him, "So what about Grandma's mother? You didn't share with her. Where is she now? And what about her mother? And what about her mother? Dad, you know many people in the Philippines are very religious and 'works oriented.' So most likely they didn't understand grace the way we do now. So are they all in hell?"

These questions really hit my dad ... hard. Where was his grandma? And where was his great-grandma? In hell? Still? (It's forever, right?)

Thing is, from what I'm aware of, my parents were the first ones in their families to convert to Protestant Christianity. That's not too far down the lineage. It's difficult to conceive of the idea that all those who "died" before them are *still* burning in hell even to this day ... and will *continue* to do so for all eternity.

Toward the end of our conversation, we talked about God's unconditional love. We even talked about the possibility that his "dead" loved ones might be with God. I didn't say, with absolute certainty, that they were. But we did talk about God being a "God of hope."

So, what if, when an "unbeliever" transitions to the "other side," God looks at this person and invites him or her to drink from the living waters?[9]

Man, I'll never forget the look on my dad's face as the conversation came to a close. With a stunned look, amazed by God's unconditional love—his heart filled with hope—and with his eyes staring at the ground, he said,

*"Now that's good news."*

And then he walked away.

• • •

So do I believe in hell? Let's see.

Everyday, people suffer from...
starvation,
drug addiction,
suicidal thoughts,
rape and sexual abuse,
guilt and condemnation,
rejection and loneliness,
and thoughts of God hating them.

You see, people often forget that there's already enough of God's children experiencing hell *now*. Why would they have to suffer more when they die, if they desire to eventually choose love?

Why not put more of our focus on the "here and now," rather than dogmatically asserting that we know exactly where people we disagree with will go when they die? Why place ourselves in that position? Who do we think we are? Do we even have a right to do such a thing?

Who knows what happens to those who don't "believe" in God during their time on earth? I personally don't think we should obsess with it nor claim to have the final word on it either. We can speculate and compare stories with what we've heard, but, still, we ultimately don't know the details until the actual day comes when we breathe our last breath.

One thing I do believe, because of my experience, is that I can trust I'll be in the arms of a loving God.

As for the details?
Let's say I'll leave those up to God.

Am I giving people false hope?
Let me answer it this way:

Once I transition over into the next life,

I'd rather be guilty of *overestimating* God's love rather than *underestimating* it.

SEVEN

# SATAN:
# THE OTHER SCAPEGOAT

*"The devil made me do it."*
**—FLIP WILSON**

*"In many ways. the Church seems to hate evil*
*more than it loves good or even God."*
**—CARLTON PEARSON**

*I have found a creature more powerful than God.*

Too hard to believe? You might be thinking, "Who can be more powerful than the *all-powerful* God?"

But wait a minute, maybe I shouldn't take too much credit for my recent discovery. I think a lot of Christians have already found this powerful creature before I did. In fact, they talk about this creature a whole lot.

The creature's name? Ready? Here goes:

It's *Satan.* Yup, that's right. *Satan.*

Actually, Satan goes by a lot of other names as well:

Lucifer (his old name)
The Devil
Beelzebub
The Beast
Prince of Darkness
Stepmother (I'm kidding)

But let's stick with "Satan" or "the Devil" for now.

Why would I say Satan is more powerful than God? Well, just listen to the things many Christians say about him. And based on what they say, I'm not even exactly sure whether they *overestimate* Satan or *underestimate* him. Or maybe they do a bit of both—

which is why it can be so darn confusing at times.

You see, according to many Christians, Satan is ...
God's greatest enemy.
Ruler over the flames of hell.
Torturing sinners for all eternity.
Eternally at war with the forces of good.
And tempting good people on earth to sell their souls
to him.

Now, that's an extremely powerful being,
don't you think?

A Christian could respond,
"But God is still more powerful than Satan."

Well then, I'm not finished yet.

Satan ...
gets more people into hell than God
gets people into heaven.
Kills millions of people everyday with
sickness and disease.
Controls the weather and sends "natural" disasters.
Seems to answer requests a lot faster than God.
Has gotten Hollywood more fascinated with him.
And does "miracles" to lead people astray.

Should I keep going? OK, I will.

I often get asked whether or not Satan can read our minds. Can he? Well, many Christians seem to think so. But think about it. If he can do such a thing, then doesn't it seem like Satan is *omniscient* like God, too?

I mean, even if he doesn't know the future per se, knowing almost everything in the *present* seems to be pretty impressive.

And not only does Satan have a sort of quasi-divine omniscience, he seems to have another divine attribute as well.

Check this out. Not only does he tempt *you* and *me* to "sin," but if you look up from reading for a moment, and look at all the people around you, Satan, amazingly so, is also tempting *all* of those people you're looking at (and others around the world) at the same time as well.

So if he's capable of doing that (which is really impressive), then doesn't it seem like Satan is *omnipresent* like God, too?

• • •

It's ironic though, because I've heard many Christians speak with a sense of authority and say, "Satan is already defeated! He has no power over you!"

But by the way some Christians interpret certain events, and how people tend to talk about Satan, it sure doesn't look like he's defeated. It actually looks like he has a huge influence over people and situations. I mean, just look at all the horrible crap happening around the world today (and in previous generations).

As I started reflecting on everything I'd been taught about Satan, and also observing the way Christians talk about this "defeated foe," I finally started to "see" things more clearly.

Satan has become, to many Christians, the *ultimate* evil being—the fierce opponent of God—the one who is behind every evil thing.

You see, in the past, I simply referred to Satan as a fallen angel. He was a good angel gone bad—a creature lower than God. But when I later discovered what he was responsible for (by the way many religious folks describe him), he had to be something more than simply a fallen angel.

Now I know Christians claim to believe in one God, but everything I was taught about Satan didn't add up to that belief.

Rather, Christianity seemed more *dualistic*.

Although most Christians wouldn't profess this—their words, beliefs, and actions do seem to indicate that Satan has become God's equal (if not greater) rival. He has become *deified*.

Should I dare say it?

Satan has become Christianity's *other* God.[1]

Is that true?

Is Satan even real?

Is he the product of our imagination? Or have we misunderstood who or what Satan is altogether?

• • •

We know the story.

Satan was once a good angel in heaven named Lucifer. He was involved in music, a worship leader if you will. But because of his greatness, he became proud and desired to be God. He led a heavenly revolt against God and one third of the angels chose to rebel with him. But God didn't put up with their crap. He cast Satan and his angels out of heaven. And since then, there's been this cosmic battle between good and evil.

Oh yeah, how can I forget? According to some inter-pretations of the narrative, Satan and his fallen angels, who are by the way God's creation, are unable to be redeemed and reconciled back to God. In other words, there's no salvation for them. They'll be lost forever. *Why?* Some of you might be wondering.

Well, we're told, that's just the way the story goes.

What are we to make of this story of Satan and his fallen angels? Is it true? And is it a good story?

Several years ago I began questioning this cosmic entity named Satan because, believe it or not, like God, Satan played a huge part in my life. And what I discovered about him was ... well ... eye-opening.

As with other things found in the Bible (God and hell), Satan has gone through an evolution as well. He wasn't always this red dude with a long tail and pitchfork.

Throughout various periods in history, Satan has been depicted in different forms. At one time, he was an angel. Another time, he had black skin with wings like a dragon, or he was a serpent, or looked like a goat. At times, he was this handsome and charming man who dressed in fine clothes and "rocked" a goatee. And even these days, he still represents control, power, wealth, sex, and fun.[2]

Throughout all these transformations of Satan, what does he *really* look like?

Well, interestingly enough, he tends to take on different forms for different people.

• • •

As I started traveling and speaking across the United States in my twenties, I had seen so-called "demons" manifesting in various ways in some of our meetings. "Demonized" people would contort their bodies and begin to growl. People tormented by "evil spirits" would hear evil voices in their heads. People would get choked by "invisible hands." And people would even see evil monster-looking creatures appear on walls with blood dripping out of their mouths. In other words, a lot of crazy s%*#!

In my own life, I've had some personal experiences with what could be interpreted as "demonic." Whatever the hell they were, they were definitely scary moments for me.

But was it my mind playing tricks on me?
Were these creepy experiences based on reality?
Did I create these experiences with my thoughts?

In all honesty, throughout the years, I went back and forth asking myself these questions.

For years I was so "demon-conscious."
Let me tell you how bad it was. I'd even hesitate to tell God my struggles, because I was afraid Satan might hear me. I thought if I'd vent to God and become vulnerable, then Satan would hear of my weaknesses and use them against me somehow. Yup, it was that bad.

Actually, it was even "badder" than that.

I even believed Satan could implant "dirty" thoughts in my mind. And let me tell you, as a young boy going through puberty, trying to rebuke every single "demonic," sexual thought was pretty exhausting.

Demons were *everywhere* for goodness sake.

If my computer was acting up,
it was a demon's fault.
If I started having emotional problems,
it was the devil stopping me from doing God's work.
If there were images of demons on objects
(posters, ornaments, jewelry, etc.), then
actual demons were attached to them.

Or if I entered a new house, I had to anoint the walls and cast out the demons left there by the previous owner. Or if I went to a hotel, I had to "bind" (rebuke) the sexual demons who caused people to fornicate in the bed I was about to sleep in. Or if I did evangelism, then I had to rebuke the "territorial spirits" to make it easier for unbelievers to receive the gospel.

Demons were somehow always a step ahead of me.

• • •

I've probably read more "spiritual warfare" books than I can remember. I had to "know the enemy" like I knew the back of my hand. The books I read contained the names of demons and also techniques on how to get rid of them. So I studied different methods of exorcisms—both Protestant and Roman Catholic—figuring out the fastest ways to expel demons from people's lives, including my own.

Whenever I'd pray for the sick and cast out demons, I'd have my spiritual warfare books with me. You see, although I knew the different techniques on how to cast demons out, I had a hard time memorizing all the names of the demons that I was supposed to address whenever I'd encounter one. (That's what I was taught.) And man, it made ministering to people so complicated at times.

During times of frustration, I'd think, "There has to be an easier way." It's like I had to be an expert. And what made things even more confusing was the fact that I never read about Jesus using some of the exorcism techniques I was using.

Then, without me even realizing it, a shift happened.

• • •

In 2008, I started hearing the message of God's grace. I immersed myself in this message for several months right before I left for the Philippines to be a missionary. So it was still, in a sense, new to me.

Once I arrived to the Philippines in January 2009, all I talked about was this message of grace. Every service and meeting we had, I emphasized the goodness and love of God.

After a year of doing ministry in the Philippines, I noticed something consistently happening, which I didn't understand.

You could say it's something I saw, but also something I didn't see.

*I saw lives transforming for the better right before my eyes. But get this, I no longer saw manifestations of the demonic like I did back in America.*[3]

To some, this may be a good thing. But for me, it was confusing. At the time, I sort of believed that if you're truly preaching the "full gospel," then demons would get pissed off and begin manifesting themselves through people—right there in your meetings.

But it wasn't happening in my meetings anymore. To be honest, I actually missed it. I know, it sounds weird. But as an evangelist—as a missionary, as a minister of the gospel—seeing demons manifest made our meetings seem, to me, more powerful.

But even though I felt that way at times, I still kept my preaching focused on God's love and grace. And as usual, our meetings were still demon-manifestation-free (at least from what I could tell). I couldn't deny the positive impact this message was having on so many people's lives—including my own!

· · ·

With all this being said, and how my mind is thinking these days, I'm a firm believer that our minds have the power to *create*.

Am I saying that there are no such things as "fallen angels"? Honestly, I ultimately don't know. But what I do know is that we tend to experience what our minds *focus* on.

Is it possible that our *worldview*—the way we *perceive* things and what we *believe*—has creative power? In other words, do our thoughts *become* things?

Is it possible that we tend to act out and experience whatever our belief system is?[4]

Is it possible that "demon-conscious" folks experience more of the demonic because they expect (create) it?

Is it possible that those who are more "demon-conscious" unknowingly invite the very things they vehemently oppose—realizing that which he or she "resists, persists"?

• • •

Is it possible to interpret the Satan/Devil passages found in the Bible as being something other than (if not limited to) a fallen angel?[5]

Trust me, after looking more into this subject, I soon discovered there are other possible interpretations of *the* satan" (not the name but the title) in the Bible that many Christians aren't even aware of. Look into it yourself. Do a word study. Try understanding the original languages and historical context of the Bible to help make sense of things. In my opinion, it's extremely important to do so.[6]

• • •

I hope I'm not being misunderstood with all this. I'm not denying the reality of *evil*. I'm well aware that there's a lot of sick and twisted stuff happening all over the world. I'm also admitting there may be invisible forces, which we might not even be aware of nor understand.

But my main issue has to do with the "blame game" some people love to play. If an *external agent* (Satan or his demons) is/are always responsible for the evil we humans commit, then this is where logic enables me to question.

Let's say you screw up and do something stupid ("sin"). And let's say you have "daddy issues" and scapegoat your father. Who does your father get to blame? Let's say he has "daddy issues" as well and blames his father. And then it goes all the way down the family line ... all the way back to, let's say, Adam. (After all, we were supposedly screwed up because of Adam's sin, right?) But let's not paint Adam as the real bad guy. Who can Adam blame for his sin?

Who's left?

That's right: *Satan.*

But here's what's confusing. If Satan is responsible for all the evil in this world, then the big question is: Who tempted the pre-Satan, the good angel, Lucifer, to sin in heaven before he "sinned" and "fell"?

Was God the external tempter to Lucifer? The other angels? I know a lot of Christians won't even go there.

So, well, I guess I won't either.

No matter who (or what) the source of evil is, I guess this topic is important to me because it's easy to scapegoat the Devil and/or demons. "The Devil made me do it" has let a lot of people off the hook. Sadly, Satan has been abused by many Christians, who make him solely responsible for some of *their* scandals.

Poor Satan.

Along these same lines of thinking, I've also seen people demonize their enemies. This happens more times than I'd like to admit. Once we accuse people of being "of the Devil," then it becomes easy to justify any violence against them. And sadly, throughout history, this mentality has given people permission to do evil things (fighting wars, burning heretics and "witches" at the stake, etc.) toward those they oppose because "they are not of God."

But who knows?
What if some of them were actually "of God"?

• • •

We must be very careful, not just with our thinking, but also with our language. I've seen both the good and bad with so-called "deliverance ministries." In my observation, some of the methods I've seen these ministries use seem more bondage-making than bondage-breaking.

Take for example, someone struggling with depression. If a "deliverance minister" tells the depressed person it's caused by the "spirit of depression," then that *thought* can eventually creep into the person's subconscious.

The depressed person might end up saying, "Uh oh, I have a demon. How do I get it out?" (Imagine yourself thinking you have a monster inside you!) And if the person keeps feeding on those thoughts, I believe, it can begin to manifest in his or her life.

• • •

Instead of limiting "the satan"
to the status of a fallen angel,
what if our understanding can be much broader?

What if something "satanic" could be referring to ...
fear itself,
the dark side of humanity,
destructive behaviors and addictions,
the use of violence and scapegoating,
any adversary (whether human or angelic),
or even demonic structures, governments,
and institutions?

In all honesty, I'm still thinking things through.

One thing I do know about myself is this: *I am willing to let go of any idea once I begin to realize it may have been a lie—especially if it leads to an unhealthy mindset or behavior.*

So what or who do you believe Satan is? Well, if you haven't made up your mind about it yet, or if this chapter has given you some food for thought, then I encourage you to do the same. Investigate this topic even more.

My challenge for all Christians is this: Take your focus *off of Satan (and evil)*, and put your focus *back on Christ (and love)*.

Don't ever keep your mind focused on the negative. It's not healthy. Trust me. Because if you keep focusing on evil, then I believe evil will never stop. So focus on the positive things in life instead.

And yes, I know, after everything I've shared,
I could still be wrong.

But hey, all I'm letting people know is that,
once I stopped being so demon-conscious,
*life for me ...*
*has been a whole lot better.*

EIGHT

# INTERFAITH: BUILDING BRIDGES

*"My humanity is bound up in yours.*
*for we can only be human together."*
**—DESMOND TUTU**

*"We may know who we are or we may not.*
*We may be Muslims. Jews or Christians but until*
*our hearts become the mould for every heart*
*we will see only our differences."*
**—RUMI**

*God cannot be owned.*

For most of my life, I believed God could.

God, in my mind, belonged to the Christians. We were, supposedly, the only ones who truly knew God.

We "had" God in our lives.

It was my God versus your god.
God is for us but God is against you.

It was us versus them.
It was my religion versus your religion.

Sadly, for many years, I suffered from a *religious superiority complex* and didn't even know it. The more "religious" (legalistic) I became, the more it worsened. You see, not only did I criticize and judge those of other faiths, but I also criticized and judged those within the Christian faith because they didn't hold to my particular "brand" of Christianity.

I honestly thought that I, and only those who agreed with me, had the *true* Christianity.

False religion impaired my vision for years.

It taught me how to s-e-p-a-r-a-t-e.
It taught me how to create WALLS.

The only group of people who belonged to God, in my eyes, got smaller and smaller and smaller.

And well ... so did ... *my* God.

But my eyes have been opened.

I can finally "see."

The truth is: Christians do not have a monopoly on God. They never have. They never will. Why? God is not that small.

In fact, no particular religion has a monopoly on God because, well, God is just that BIG.

We all carry labels, don't we?

"I'm a Christian."
"I'm a Muslim."
"I'm a Buddhist."
"I'm a skeptic."
"I'm an atheist."
"Don't call me anything."

Labels are inevitable.
They help us identify and narrow things down, so I'm not against them to some degree.

But then again, labels are also a two-edged sword. They *help* people, but they also *hurt* people. They *unite* people, but they also *divide* people.

Religious labels are a two-edged sword as well. They can give someone a sense of identity. But they can also, unfortunately, exclude the "other."[1]

• • •

I personally believe many people around the world end up adopting the religion of their parents (or whoever raised them). It's no surprise, really. It's easy to recognize that particular religions are more dominant in certain parts of the world.

For instance,
If you're born in America,
you're most likely a Protestant Christian.
If you're born in China,
you're most likely a Buddhist.
If you're born in the Middle East,
you're most likely a Muslim.
If you're born in the Philippines,
you're most likely a Roman Catholic.

Of course, it's not always the case. There are exceptions. But we can't deny the influence our surrounding environments have on us. Even if one doesn't claim to be religious, he or she is most likely surrounded by religious people and beliefs of a certain culture.

As for myself, I grew up Protestant—a charismatic evangelical Protestant. (See how labels help identify?) It's what my parents were. They wanted to raise me in their version of Christianity. It's all I knew as a child.

• • •

Growing up as a Christian, I can honestly say that I loved people of other faiths. As a matter of fact, some of them even became my closest friends. There was so much we had in common.

We watched the same movies,
had the same hobbies,
laughed at the same jokes,
and loved the same food.

But in spite of our similarities, and even though I loved them, I always had these thoughts in the back of my mind:

*I need to save them.*
*They're going to hell.*
*I need to convert them to Christianity*
*before they die.*

It's interesting, because they could've been some of the most loving people in the world (and many of them were definitely nicer than me at times), but my religion taught me that they were still "out of Christ."

Sure, they can belong to *me* as friends but, according to what religion taught me, they will never, ever belong to *God* until they believed in God the way I did.

• • •

As a Filipino-American, I've had my share of racism. Sure, I was a human being like everyone else, but, sadly, some people still saw me as "the other."

Let's face it.
I have a flat face,
slanted eyes,
dark skin,
and I eat "weird" food. (And yes, I have been asked the "Do you eat dog?" question several times.)

It's not the nicest feeling in the world to be seen as different—at least in the inferior sense. Sure, "different" in the sense of uniqueness is awesome. But "different" in the sense of being excluded, looked down upon, or not being accepted is ... well ... not so awesome.

For those people who focused on racial differences because of my Filipino nationality, there was a sense of "separation" between me and others who didn't look like me.

*Why couldn't I be accepted by my fellow Americans?*
I wondered.

Sure, our Filipino language is different. And sure, our food is different (and good I might add). And sure, our traditional clothing is different.

But, hey, I'm still a person ... *just like everyone else.*

And being a person—a human being—I have emotions ... *just like everyone else.* And rejection, well, let's say it's not that great of a feeling for someone to experience at such a young age (or any age for that matter).

Like my experiences with racism,
I wonder if we create the same feelings
for those we judge of other faiths.

What happens when I tell a Muslim
he or she is not accepted by God?
What happens when I tell a Mormon
he or she is not God's child?
What happens when I tell a Jew
he or she is not "saved"?

What about you? Have you ever truly sought to understand those of other faiths? Have you ever sat down with someone and asked how this person came to embrace his or her particular religion?

Not to criticize it.
Not to condemn it.

But to listen. To learn. To understand.

Isn't it humbling to be reminded of the fact that everyone has a story?

You have a story.
I have a story.

It's so easy to condemn a person of a different religion. But wait until he or she becomes your close friend. Then what?

• • •

I remember back in Bible school I took a class on the religion of Islam. My homework assignments were to read the entire Qur'an and go to mosques every week to share the gospel and "defend the faith." So I did.

I read every book I could get my hands on about Islam before I went to the mosques. My classmates and I were told that many Muslims were knowledgeable of Christianity and also very argumentative. So I read their holy book and studied their beliefs and arguments.

I did my best to "understand" them.

I'll never forget the first time I went to a mosque with some friends. I was ready to debate. I asked a lot of questions to the Muslim we met at the door. I acted like I was interested in him and his religion, but, in reality, I was only looking for an opportunity to share and defend the Christian gospel.

"Hold on," he said,
"Let me get the rest of our scholars."

Then, out of nowhere,
several men entered the room. All of them sat down in a row of chairs in front of us, as though we were having some sort of panel discussion.

But my friends and I were ready. We weren't going to back down. We argued back and forth with the scholars. We quoted Bible verses, used persuasive logic, and referenced historical events to demonstrate our religion as better. We used everything at our disposal to "defend the Christian faith."

Toward the end of the "debate," one of the Muslims said they had never met any Christians like us before. Our answers surprised them. They felt challenged. And I was flattered.

"Of course they felt challenged," I thought.
"After all, our religion is better than theirs."

Then we thanked them for their time and we went our merry way.

My friends and I did this type of activity for several weeks. We did it so often I felt like I "knew" what Muslims were all about.

But all of that was about to change. My friends and I went to another mosque one Friday evening. This time it was different. The Muslim we met at the entrance was not aggressive or argumentative at all. In fact, he was very kind. He even told us, as he gave us a tour of the mosque, that Islam was a religion of peace.

*"A religion of peace? Yeah right!"* With a skeptical look on my face I said, "How is it a religion of peace when your Qur'an is filled with violence? And how is it a religion of peace after what happened on 9/11?"

"Not all Muslims are the same," he replied.[2]

Then he introduced us to one of his friends. (No, it wasn't to debate us.) To my surprise, his friend was very kind as well. In fact, he shared a powerful testimony of how his life dramatically changed. He said he used to be hooked on a lot of drugs in his past, but when he became Muslim, Allah (the Arabic word for God) changed his life.

Interesting.

Listening to him reminded me of those typical "churchy" testimonies you often hear in Christian meetings.

Honestly, when I heard the guy share his testimony, deep down, I was so happy for him. After all, he seemed so genuine. His life was better. He was very positive. And he definitely seemed like he wanted to inspire us with his story.

But still, there was this other part of me thinking, "He's wrong."

Rather than *celebrating* his victory over drug-addiction, I *challenged* his religion—the religion which helped him get through tough times.

Why?

*All for the sake of protecting my religion.*

• • •

During that same period, I went to a temple one day to "evangelize" Buddhists. I was amazed by the temple's beauty. And the people, well, they looked so peaceful—even more peaceful than a lot of Christians I knew.[3]

But once again, I had to look past all that. I had a

mission—an agenda. I had to share my faith and try to convert Buddhists to Christianity. It was, in the end, my main goal for befriending them.[4]

As I walked around the temple, I found a lady who was willing to dialogue with me. My initial reaction was that she was sweet and friendly.

"I used to be a Christian," she said. "But I became a Buddhist because they seem more loving." Her words caught me off guard for a moment. She, a Buddhist, exemplified the love she was talking about.

But, once again, rather than *celebrating* her faith-journey of discovering love, I challenged her "false religion of false love."

*Once again,*
*all for the sake of protecting my religion.*

• • •

I often hear many Christians say,
"It's not about religion. It's about *relationship*."

If what they say is true, then why do those same Christians get uncomfortable when I mention "Christianity" is not the only way to God?

After all, did Jesus tell his disciples, "Hey, guys, once

I go back to the Father, do me a favor. I want you to name a religion after me called 'Christianity' so people can enter it in order to get to God."

I doubt it.

To me, Jesus didn't come to bring a religion. In fact, it actually seems like he came for just the opposite—to expose it and to offer us a better way.

Jesus came to reveal the heart of God. What he had was a relationship with God—an intimate one—one which went beyond rules or a statement of faith. Jesus came to show us the way of love.

Jesus showed us how to love the "unlovable,"
to accept the "unacceptable,"
and to forgive the "unforgivable."

*That is the way of Jesus.*

Jesus pointed people to the truth. It wasn't for them to embrace a particular religion. Truth helps people experience a vitality and quality of life. Truth removes the lies of fear and separation.

In short, knowing the truth sets people free.
Or better stated, truth let's people know
they are *already free.*

What if life is less about having to follow a particular religion, and more about having to look more like Christ, which transcends beyond American (or whatever country you're from) Christianity?

What if we stop arguing for which religion is the best and start focusing on the best in every person?

You see, every person is on a journey. For goodness sake, look at me. I'm already in my thirties. I grew up Christian. And I'm still learning about God.

Why can't we look at those of other faiths the same way? I'm just as human as anyone else. You're just as human as anyone else. Aren't we all learning and unlearning things?

Think about it.

We were all born into this world
at a certain place and time.
We all inherited some beliefs
from those who raised us.
And we're all trying to figure out
this thing called "life."
(For a lot of us, it hasn't been an easy road either.)

Don't get me wrong, I'm not saying all religions teach exactly the same thing. And I'm not saying everything a person believes is true.

*But truth is truth ... no matter where it's found.*

So just as a Buddhist can know truth, a Buddhist can also believe falsehoods. And just like the Buddhist, a Christian can know truth, but a Christian can also believe a lot of falsehoods.

That's what *all* people experience.

People are people. So we are no different in that sense. We are all limited and growing in our understanding of the Infinite.

• • •

Sadly, sometimes our biggest "enemies" are those within our own religion. For me, the most heartless emails, comments, and confrontations I receive are from Christians.[5]

They have ...
damned me to hell,
"broken fellowship" with me,
and have called me unkind names.

All because my beliefs are *different*
than some of theirs.

And here's the irony:
These hateful Christians are supposedly the only ones

who are "saved" and on their way to heaven because they are simply just that—Christians. Really?

Something is definitely wrong with this mentality, which is why I believe our views of God need to change.

Because,
once we end up *believing* in an exclusive God,
then we end up *being* exclusive too.

• • •

I've heard many Christians say, "We are all God's *creation*, but we are not all God's *children*. One must believe in Jesus in order to become God's child. Until then, people are on their way to hell."

Is that true?

Let me ask you this ... are you a parent?
Can you honestly look into your child's eyes
and believe such a perspective?

But here's the response I usually get
from Christians:

"Well, babies are the exception to the rule. They are God's children while they're young. They haven't reached the 'age of accountability.' So if they die any time before that they will go to heaven."

Really? So let me get this straight:
All babies are God's children.
But once they reach the "age of accountability,"
they are no longer God's children.
But once they "believe,"
they suddenly become God's children again?

Huh? So complicated.

Is it possible that everyone is God's child—but some,
for whatever reason, just don't know it yet? Is it possible we are all one with the Divine Source—God—the
ground of being?

Think about it.

What if a Muslim took a bullet for you?
What if a Hindu jumped on a bomb for you?
What if a Buddhist lent you money in times
of need?
What if an atheist pushed you out of the way
from an oncoming train?
What if?

Are those things not love?

As I mentioned in another chapter, the late Mother
Teresa said, "Where there is love, there is God."

Love has no boundaries.

So why create them?

• • •

Several years ago my wife and I watched a powerful documentary called *The Human Experience.*[6] The film tells the story of several young men who travel certain parts of the world to answer the question: *What does it mean to be human?*

The scene which had the biggest impact on me was when the men visited a leper colony in Africa. In the film, you'll see people with missing fingers, toes, teeth, and also people with blind eyes. Slowly but surely, their bodies were decaying and being eaten away. They were looked upon by others as though they had a curse. They were segregated from the rest of the population—even from their own family and friends.

They were considered the *outcasts* of society.

During this particular scene, one of the lepers starts talking to the American travelers. The leper has no feet. He was abandoned by his own family. And his own son doesn't even look at him as his father anymore.

I guess you could say he had it pretty bad.

But, as you see in the film, this leper is ... *happy.*

This leper ... this person ... *this human being* ...
looks to the Americans with a big smile and says,
"You are not afraid of us.
We are the same.
You are my brother.
We are here to love everybody.
And we are happy."

At that moment I wanted to tear up. I looked to my
wife and said, "I see it. I see it so clearly now."

I doubt any of these lepers were evangelical Christians. In fact, I don't know if any of them claim any
particular religion at all. But you know what?

Even if they did, it honestly doesn't matter to me.

*Because I saw God in them.*

I saw love in their smiles.
I heard love in their words.
I felt love in my heart.

Religion or no religion,
they are walking on a certain path in this life. What
they're living is *their human experience.* And I wasn't
going to try and take it away from them.

I can't imagine Jesus going up to any of these lepers saying, "None of you are God's children.
None of you are my brothers and sisters.
Not until you become a Christian."

I just ... can't.

• • •

All life is *sacred*.
We are all *connected*.
We are all *one*.

I finally reached a point in my life where I can look into another person's eyes—a Buddhist, a Hindu, a skeptic, or whoever—it doesn't matter—and who I see is ...
another *human being* ...
made in God's image.

I see my precious brother,
my precious sister,
God's child.
I see ... me.

Do you want to see the face of God? Then look around you. Every human being, no matter what religion he or she may embrace, is God's masterpiece.

Whatever we do to each other, we must remember, we actually do it *unto* God.[7]

It's no longer "us versus them" anymore.
Those days are long gone for me.

*It's only us.*

What I'm asking you to do is to look *beyond* a person's religion and into his or her heart. And to remember that everyone has a story.

You have yours.
I have mine.
People have theirs.

And we're all headed somewhere.

But no matter where we're at in life, or wherever we're going, I believe God is not far from any of us.[8]

What I'm asking for ...
my dear brother ... my dear sister ...
God's precious child ... is if we can join hands,
focus on our similarities
rather than our differences,
and walk this journey ...
*together.*

NINE

# CHURCH:
# A BEAUTIFUL MESS

*"It is difficult to get a man to understand something, when his salary depends upon his not understanding it."*
**—UPTON SINCLAIR**

*"The person who says it cannot be done should not interrupt the person doing it."*
**—CHINESE PROVERB**

*So where do you go to church?*

If you're a Christian, you've probably been asked this question before. It shouldn't be a surprise. It is, after all, part of the everyday Christian lingo. Both "going" to church and being a Christian seem to go hand-in-hand for a lot of people.

But haven't you also heard the phrase "we are the church"? Well, I have. Ask Christians what the "church" really is and most of them would say,

"We are."

But, strangely enough, aren't these the same folks who also ask you where you go to church?

So which is it?

Is "church" a place you go to?
Or is "church" *us—people*?

Would it ever be appropriate to ask someone, "Hey, so where do you go to *yourself*?"

Of course, I'm joking. Sort of. I guess what I'm trying to say is that I think a lot of people are confused about the whole idea of what church is really all about. I know I was for most of my life.

For years I believed "church" was a place you go to—like an event, a Bible study, or even a building. And for some reason, I guess I didn't put two and two together. Because whenever someone would ask me directly to define "church," I'd say it's *us—people*. But then again, the rest of my language and actions said otherwise.

Now, before I continue,
let me put a disclaimer out there.

I am *not* against the church.

I love the church. Plain and simple.

But with the heavy emphasis on "going" to church coming from many religioust folks, it makes a world of difference how one defines it.

• • •

I grew up "going" to church. Well, let me be more specific. I grew up going to an *institutional* church. (So every time I talk about church being a location, this is what I mean.) This is, after all, what most people are familiar with anyway.

You see, church these days is basically a system—a machine—where religious folks come together for a service/meeting. Interestingly enough, church services seem to be pretty much the same format no matter where you attend.

During the service, there are:
announcements,
"praise and worship,"
a collection of "tithes,"
a sermon by the pastor,
and a benediction.[1]

Of course, some churches change it up a bit by adding things here and there. But for the most part, programs and rituals are usually the things which sustain these kinds of meetings.

Looking back, I must admit—no matter what church I served at—it ran like a business. Every week my staff and I had meetings about programs, programs, programs. Oh, yes, did I forget to mention programs?

Sure, there was the occasional, "How are you doing?" from fellow leaders, but the main focus was still the same:

*Programs.*

To be honest, as a church leadership team, we had to *entertain* people. Now, there's nothing necessarily wrong with entertaining people. Entertainment is ... well ... entertainment.

But I really wonder, would certain communities still meet together without all the fancy schmancy entertainment stuff (skits, cool power-points, rockin' worship team)? Or is coming together every week really about watching a religious show?

I mean, even when I did build relationships in church, what's sad is the fact that I spent more time serving people in church than serving my own family at home. I ended up neglecting my own flesh and blood, because I was too busy "serving God" in church. And you know what? I wouldn't be surprised if many pastors do (or have done) this as well.

• • •

In 2009, I became a missionary to the Philippines. And since I hardly knew anyone in the country, I hopped from one church to another.

I wanted *friends*.
I wanted a church *family*.
I wanted a place I could call *home*.

But I couldn't forget I was on a "mission." I wanted to spread the gospel all over the country. The problem was that I had no platform.

But I had a plan. For months I attended different church services to try and connect with people. I met privately with well-known pastors and taught small groups here and there. *I had connections, man!* I already had my "foot in the door," so to speak—a lot faster than those who have been climbing the "ministry ladder" for years.

I guess, for a time, things were going as planned for me, right? Well, in some ways, yes. But in some ways, no. See, there was a bit of a problem with the people I was surrounded with.

I wasn't feeling a *connection*.

I couldn't understand it. Thing is, I'm a pretty relational guy, too. I'm easy to get along with. (At least I like to think so.) And the people I met were all so nice. I didn't know what the heck was going on. Why wasn't I "clicking" with anyone?

I was even put on a pedestal by church leaders. Wherever I went, I was introduced to people as the "new missionary guy"—the "guy who does healing"—and the "preacher from America." I mean, who wouldn't want this kind of recognition?

But you know what? Screw the flattering labels. What I wanted to know was if the people really wanted to know *me*. Or were they only interested in the "titles" and "gifts" I had? I wasn't quite sure.

Several months in, for the most part, the relationships I had with people at the churches I was attending still remained surface level. None of them got too deep. Sometimes I'd be sitting in a service (bored out of my mind) thinking, "I'd rather be chillin' at Starbucks talking with someone."

I was seriously longing for *authentic* relationships.

Walking to an empty home everyday didn't make things any better. It sucked coming home to no one. I had no idea where my life was going. I had no idea who my real friends were. And I had no idea that living alone, and being thousands of miles away from my immediate family, could make me go crazy.

All these negative thoughts and feelings eventually came toppling down on me. I felt out of place. Not just within the groups of friends I'd made, but in the Philippines in general.

I felt confused. I felt extremely lonely. And a part of me wanted to go back home to America.

One night I went to bed and broke down crying. I couldn't control the tears. I started yelling in my bedroom (the benefits of living alone) apologizing to God—"I'm so sorry if I failed you as a missionary!"

In spite of all the things I had accomplished in such

a short period of time, I felt hopeless. I felt lost. And I ended up crying myself to sleep that night.

The next morning, I told God that if I wasn't going to officially join the mega churches I was helping, then I wanted to make an impact in the media in order to reach more people. I wanted to spread good news all around the country. But I had no idea how.

Surprisingly, later that afternoon, I received a text message on my phone inviting me to be a guest on a radio show.

Coincidence? Answered prayer? Whatever it was, the timing couldn't have been better.

• • •

The day of the radio interview was a huge turning point for me. I immediately connected with the people there. (It's so crazy how that happens.) And then they introduced me to more awesome people. It was like a domino effect. One thing led to another, and things started to fall into place.

Fast forward a couple months, and I ended up planting a church with a couple of my closest friends in the Philippines. We were a small group in the beginning. But that didn't last too long. Word got out that there was "this new church sharing a radical version of grace where miracles are taking place." So every week, without any fancy advertisement, new people would visit. It was pretty exciting!

The funny thing is, our church had no name. But we were eventually called "The Church With No Name" by those who heard about us. It was kind of silly, but cool at the same time. We were just a bunch of friends wanting to spread a message.

LOVE.

People kept coming to our meetings. Our group got bigger. Fast. And the dynamics of our gatherings began to change as well. In the beginning stages, when we would simply meet together, we were pretty "laid back."

But over time, when more people joined us, we ended up becoming more *structured*. We started focusing more on having a legit "praise and worship" team. And we started having formal announcements in the beginning like a typical church service.

Structured.
Formal.
Routine.

*The bigger our gatherings got,*
*the less intimate they became.*[2]

To be quite honest, I started to not like it—the less intimate part, I mean. Instead of us being a simple family who just wanted to love on people, things started becoming more ... well ... "programmatic." (There's that darn word again with "matic" attached to it.)

I eventually started to realize my understanding of church was inconsistent with what I was doing and saying. I'd always said and believed church meant people. But there I was, month after month, putting so much time and effort into a *program*, which a lot of people called "church."

Aside from our Sunday programs, some people in our church community literally spent hours and hours with each other almost everyday. We hung out in homes, bars, coffee shops, and restaurants.

Sometimes we talked about God and theology. Sometimes we didn't. No matter where we hung out, we just wanted to be together.

We got into each other's lives.
We encouraged each other.
We helped each other financially.
And we even prayed for the sick
whenever we saw the need.

But then again, we still had this Sunday program, which was somewhat fixed. It honestly started to feel out of place—well, at least for me. It was sort of like an interruption in the flow of life we were already experiencing throughout the week.

So I wondered: Was it really necessary to still have our Sunday church services?

• • •

OK, it's confession time.
I reached a point where I didn't want to go to church on Sunday anymore. Yes, me—the one people looked up to as their "pastor."[3] I didn't want to go to my own church anymore. Go figure.

I couldn't deny the feeling. It wasn't a bad feeling, really. Don't get me wrong, prior to having this feeling, I honestly had a blast having "church" for a certain period of time. But since our relationships deepened beyond the Sunday program, my feelings about it started to change. I didn't want to have a Sunday service just for the sake of having a Sunday service anymore. You know what I'm saying? It seemed to break the flow of things.

It didn't seem ... well ... *natural* anymore.

And, no, I wasn't trying to be a lazy bum either. I definitely didn't want to stop sharing life with people. And I definitely didn't want to stop sharing the gospel.

I just wanted to do things in a more—what you might call—*organic way*.

I felt God was doing something different in my heart and was wanting to reveal something new to me. But I still didn't know what to do.

I felt stuck.

I eventually picked up a book called *So You Don't Want to Go to Church Anymore*. The title says it all.[4]

The gist of the book?

It's about *being* the church
instead of *going* to church.
It's about having *authentic* relationships
instead of *ministry-based* ones.

And, well, that's what I genuinely wanted.

I remember reading the first few chapters of the book and suddenly breaking down in tears. It hit home for me, because I related to the main character of the story in so many ways.

I eventually asked my church group if they'd be willing to read the book. Thankfully, some of them did. I was very transparent and let them all know I was sort of in a dilemma.

I wasn't afraid to acknowledge I was somewhat confused with what to do next with the "ministry."

• • •

I canceled our service one Sunday afternoon and ended up talking about the book with the ones I was closest to. As expected, they all loved it. After we all went around and shared our thoughts, I talked about how I wanted to take things in a different direction. I told them I wanted to try this whole "being the church" thing.

Well, to sum up their response, it was this:
*There is no turning back.*

And, from that point on, things definitely changed. We ended up not meeting on Sundays anymore for our usual church service. But here's what's so cool.

*We still met up together.*[5]

I mean, why wouldn't we? We enjoyed each other's company. And that's what friends do, right?

We never had to ask each other, "How was your week?" because we lived as a family. We ate together, watched movies together, prayed together; you name it, we did everything together ... almost every day. (Not just on Sunday.)

Come to think of it, this new way of "doing" church wasn't new to any of us in *practice*.

It's called *living life*.

It was more real. More spontaneous. More organic. It's something I think, you know, normal people do.

You see, religion likes to make these artificial distinctions between the "secular" and the "sacred"—or the "common" and the "holy."

But what if these distinctions don't really exist? What if religion made it all up? What if it's all just a bunch of bull, which has kept people from truly enjoying God in everything?

God wants us to live fully human. The problem with religion is that it's only concerned with *part* of life.

Spirituality, on the other hand, *is* life.

*Everything is spiritual.*

• • •

I must admit, I did question myself, wondering if the direction we took was the right one. I started wondering if I failed as a church planter because, typically, when you plant something, it's supposed to grow.

Upon reflection, I realized my focus was in the wrong place. Because that's exactly what I started to see— *growth*—not necessarily in a *numerical* way of filling up pews in a church building. But it was definitely a growth in a *deep, emotional* and *relational* way.

Because our group was built on relationships, things weren't always so nice and neat as they usually are during church programs. Life did get pretty messy at times. But I guess that's the beauty of it all.

The relationships were so raw. So genuine. So real.

• • •

One time my friends and I were hanging out at a mall, and we ran into a Christian near the escalator. "Where are you going?" I asked him. "I'm going to church," he said. (Churches in shopping malls are very common in the Philippines.)

Then my friends and I turned to each other with surprise, and we simultaneously said, "Oh yeah! It's Sunday!"

We were in each other's lives so much, Sunday was just another day.

• • •

I'll never forget a day when my friends and I hung out at a park. One of the girls started a conversation about what she'd been learning concerning God's grace. It wasn't long before one of the guys decided to open up about something he was struggling with. He had a deep secret, which he couldn't keep to himself. He felt the need to confess.

And, no, it wasn't something like, "I forgot to put the toilet seat down" or "I'm addicted to video games." It was something you wouldn't usually hear someone confess in a church setting. (At least I hadn't.) He felt so safe with us. And that's all that really mattered to him ... and to us.

*He felt safe.* (That, my friend, is a big deal.)

As we sat and listened to him share his struggle, he kept cursing and being hard on himself. He looked embarrassed. He couldn't even make eye contact with any of us. We all saw how difficult it was for him to be this vulnerable.

Then, out of nowhere, one of our friends listening sat next to the guy sharing and put his arm around his shoulder. Then I turned my head to look at the girls in the group. I wanted to catch their reactions to what was being confessed.

And what I saw was amazing.

Not one person listening during the confession looked disgusted with the confessor. Only smiles of love and gestures of comfort.

No condemnation.
No self-righteous judgment.
No rebuking.
From anyone.

Moved by everyone's reactions, I turned to the guy who was sharing and said, "We're not here to fix you. We're just here to love you." (Why kick him while he's already feeling down?)

Then I uttered the most spiritual words you could ever say to a person who's hurting:

"Let's eat."

We all broke out in laughter. We didn't close in prayer. And we didn't even quote a Bible verse to him.[6] We all just stood up and started walking.

*Together.*
*As a family.*

As we walked together, with arms around each other (as buddies do), the guy who confessed his secret to us said, "Thank you for loving me."

Those words hit me like a ton of bricks.

Man, that night, on the way home, I sat in the back seat of my friend's car and my eyes began to tear up. Moved by what just happened, a thought came to mind,

"This is what it's all about. It's about being real with each other. It's about loving each other."

*No matter what.*

I'm not saying we did nothing to help him that day. Healing takes time. But true healing, I believe, comes through *loving relationships*. That's what he needed. And that's what we gave him.

• • •

A community of grace is what people need. It's so easy to put on an I'm-OK-mask because you don't want anyone thinking you're not "spiritual." It can feel embarrassing to share your deepest and darkest secrets to just one person—let alone an entire group.

I'm not saying you should share all the "skeletons in your closet" with everyone. *Trust is very important.* Nobody likes to be judged or be looked down upon.

No one does.

But isn't it interesting that the place many religious folks call a "spiritual hospital" (church) for the "spiritually sick," usually ends up being a place where everyone looks healthy? So instead of being a place where we can "be ourselves," the church usually ends up being a place where we pretend everything is okay.

Truth is, life is not always okay. Everyone has a story. Deep down, beneath the facades, behind the masks, there are *real people*. And with real people, come *real problems*.

No one wants to give his or her heart to someone fake. No one wants to expose his or her wounds to those who don't really care. If people aren't real with themselves first, then they won't be real with anyone else. That's just the way it is. "Being real" is what creates real intimacy among people—not religious programs.

• • •

Look, if you *do* experience authentic relationships and love in an institutional church, then cool. Stay. But if you *don't* experience those things there, well, I don't think you should feel guilty about it. You can choose to stay or choose to leave. It's really up to you. What would benefit you the most at this time in your life?

Was going to church a complete waste for me all

those years? I don't think so.

In an institutional church, I have...
met lifelong friends,
heard inspiring sermons,
seen relief centers after a natural disaster,
seen homeless people given a place to live,
and seen programs help the poor, the broken,
and the lost.

In other words, there's always something good to point out in the things we constructively criticize.

Then again, we all have our own experiences. And we all need different things at different times.

So if there's one big point I want to make in all of this, it's this:

Stop *focusing* on GOING to church.
Start BEING the church.

Cry.
Laugh.
Play.
Agree.
Disagree.
Inspire.
Celebrate.
Encourage.

Live.
Love.

*Just be yourselves.*

Because deep down,
no one is looking for perfect people.
We're looking for *real* ones.

Quit trying to "go" to church.
Quit trying to "do" church.
Stop trying.

Just BE.

TEN

# LETTING GO
## —CONCLUSION—

*"And still, after all this time,*
*the Sun has never said to the Earth,*
*'You owe me.'*
*Look what happens with love like that.*
*It lights up the sky."*
**—RUMI**

Inspire.

That's what I'm hoping this book will do for you. I'm hoping my personal thoughts, questions, and stories will help inspire your own.

This is a story about my journey.
And, well, you're on your own journey.

It's not about having to always have all the right answers anyway. No one needs to have this stuff all figured out. No one can.

Give up the desire to know it all.
Be willing to embrace mystery.

Sometimes having legitimate questions is enough to help us along the way.

The best thing we can do
is to keep moving forward.

I'm an *optimist*. I don't believe fear-based religion has the final word about our lives. It's only part of our story—but it doesn't have to be the end of it.

There's an *awakening to love* happening all over the world. Those finding the courage to help others are no longer remaining silent.

They shouldn't.
And neither should you.

If your heart is to help others experience true freedom from fear-based religion, then don't be afraid to speak up. Even if no one around you does, you still can.

*Somebody has to say something.*

Be a voice for the people.
But don't just speak it,
live it.

Let your responses and reactions to those whom you disagree with reflect your message. Your actions speak louder than your words.

No matter where you stand theologically
on all the issues raised in this book,
my main desire for you is this:

To love freely.
And to live honestly.

•  •  •

I'd like to end this book with a funny story my wife, Remy, shared with me.[1]

Several years ago in Thailand,

my wife decided to go for a swim in the ocean. It was her first time going snorkeling, and she was really excited about it.

As she slowly walked beyond the shore and into the water, she was soon to discover what awaited her.

Once she dipped herself beneath the surface of the water, she became fascinated with all the colors and movements of the creatures who swam in unison.

But as she stretched out her foot to try and stand, there was a bit of a problem. She couldn't feel the ground. So she panicked.

Although she wanted to overcome the waters, she didn't realize how far she had drifted from the shore. (Did I forget to mention she didn't know how to swim?)

So there she was ... struggling for dear life ... her arms flapping hard against the water, trying to reach something to grab onto.

But still, no one came to her rescue.

All she heard from a distance was her friend laughing. In her mind she thought, "I'm gasping for air and my friend is laughing?!"

"You're wearing a life jacket!" her friend yelled. "Nothing can beat the force of buoyancy!"

*The force of buoyancy! Of course!*

Instead of coming to Remy's rescue, her friend just laughed and laughed away, because she knew Remy couldn't drown, even if she tried.

Coming into that *awareness,*
Remy stopped struggling for dear life.

So there was Remy in the ocean ... *feeling free.*

Laughing.
Floating.
Trusting.

With a bit of self-assurance and a couple of deep breaths, she "flapped" herself back to shore.

Something insightful hit her that day. She realized how this whole experience could possibly liberate every area of her life. Because of the life jacket she was wearing, she didn't even have to try and keep herself afloat.

She simply had to stop,
*let go,*
and trust in her life jacket.

Like Remy's story, you have nothing to fear. You're not going to "drown" in the pain of your past. Recognize that today can be a *new day* for you.

We're all swimming in this ocean we call "life." There's so much to explore, so much to see, and so much to learn.

*You're safe in God.*

So take a deep breath.

Cease striving.
Cease self-effort.
Cease struggling.

Trust that God is keeping you afloat.
All you need to do is...



LET GO.

# ENDNOTES

**PREFACE: A New Language, A New World**

1. I highly recommend Brian McLaren's *A New Kind of Christianity: Ten Questions That Are Transforming the Faith* (New York: HarperCollins, 2010) and also Rob Bell's *Velvet Elvis: Repainting the Christian Faith* (Grand Rapids, MI: Zondervan, 2005). Both books have done a great job at helping people see Christianity in a different and more positive way. I'm simply adding to the conversation with my perspective.
2. Thanks to the power of social media. Because of Youtube, Facebook, Twitter and the whole blogosphere world, many people now have a platform for their voices to be heard.

**1) GOD: I No Longer Believe**

1. When I say "charismatic," what I mean is a person who tends to emphasize the "supernatural" gifts of the Holy Spirit. Many (not all) whom I've met sounded like they had an intimate relationship with God, where they talk back-and-forth with him. A common thing to hear them say is, "God told me ..."
2. This is from A.W. Tozer's book *The Knowledge of the Holy: The Attributes of God: Their Meaning in the Christian Life* (New York: HarperCollins, 1961), 1.
3. I highly recommend Darin Hufford's book *The Misunderstood God* (Newbury Park, CA: Windblown Media, 2009). It has opened up my eyes in so many ways to the love of God.
4. Today, "worship" is commonly understood as singing songs to God. Or it is usually referred to as the "slow songs" during the time of singing to God while "praise" refers to the "fast songs." To me, worship is a lifestyle. It's everything we do.
5. For more thoughts on this, check out Paul Tillich's writing—specifically his three-volume *Systematic Theology*. I'm

grateful for John Shelby Spong's books *Why Christianity Must Change or Die* (Australia: HarperCollins, 1998), *A New Christianity For A New World* (Australia: HarperCollins, 2001), and John A.T. Robinson's *Honest to God* (Philadelphia, PA: The Westminister Press, 1963) for helping me appreciate the writings of Tillich even more.

6. I recommend the writings of Matthew Fox. He has two great books, which deal with God being in all things. One is *Original Blessing: A Primer in Creation Spirituality* (Santa Fe, NM: Bear & Company, 1983) and the other is *The Coming of the Cosmic Christ* (San Francisco, CA: Harper & Row, 1998).

7. I think the best book out there on learning how to live in the "now" and be aware of Presence is Eckhart Tolle's *The Power of Now: A Guide to Spiritual Enlightenment* (Novato, CA: New World Library, 1999). This book is destined to be a classic.

## 2) BIBLE: The Paper God

1. I found Raymund Schwager's quote in Eric Seibert's *Disturbing Divine Behavior: Troubling Old Testament Images of God* (Minneapolis, MN: Fortress Press, 2009), Kindle edition.

2. The book which inspired much of this chapter, and probably the best book I've read to date against the doctrine of inerrancy, has to be Thom Stark's *The Human Faces of God: What Scripture Reveals When It Gets God Wrong (and Why Inerrancy Tries To Hide It)* (Eugene, OR: Wipf & Stock, 2011). The book is definitely a beast, in my opinion. His arguments are very persuasive.

3. Leviticus 25:44–46.

4. A whole bunch of plagues can be found in the book of Exodus chapters 3-11.

5. Joshua 6-11 and 1 Samuel 15.

6. Genesis 6-9.

7. 1 Sam 16:14-16, 23.

8. Lev 26:29; Jer 19:9; Ezek 5:9-10.

9.  Genesis 22:1-3.
10. Isaiah 45:7; Amos 3:6.
11. Malachi 3:6; Hebrews 13:8.
12. Genesis 9.
13. See Deuteronomy 20:16–19 and Joshua 6-11.
14. Psalm 137:9 (NIV).
15. See Colossians 3:22 and Ephesians 6:5.
16. See Matthew 18:1-10; 19:14 and Galatians 3:28.
17. In *A New Kind of Christianity: Ten Questions That Are Transforming the Faith* (New York: HarperCollins, 2010). Brian McLaren has an entire section on the Bible, which is worth reading.

## 3) GRACE: Giving Up

1.  Altar calls are usually invitations for people to come forward publicly during church services to either "give their lives to Christ" or to "rededicate" themselves to him.
2.  Joseph Prince's book *Destined to Reign: The Secret to Effortless Success, Wholeness and Victorious Living* (Tulsa, OK: Harrison House, 2007) had a huge impact on me when I first read it back in 2008. His book opened up my eyes to the whole idea that preaching the law empowers people to "sin." Although the book teaches penal substitution, which is something I strongly disagree with, I'm so grateful for the many insights of grace I've received from him.
3.  1 John 4:19 (NIV) emphasis mine.
4.  His name is Jesus. This statement is found in Luke 7:47.

## 4) GOSPEL: The Good News Just Got Gooder

1.  I'm thankful for this insight I received from Bruce Wauchope who said something along the same lines in his video series "What is the Gospel?" (Online video clip. *YouTube*. 10 Jan. 2010.) It is one of the most insightful presentations of the gospel I have ever heard.

2.  Kruger, C. Baxter. *The Parable of the Dancing God* (Jackson, MS: Perichoresis Press, 1994), 6.
3.  1 John 4:8.
4.  Just to clarify, my wife wasn't like this with everyone. Unfortunately, she grew up legalistically and "kissed dating goodbye" which made her put a guard up at times with guys. But the first day I met her, I knew she was really a softy inside.
5.  I first heard it put this way from a message by C. Baxter Kruger called *In* (Online audio clip. Perichoresis, Inc. 15 Oct. 2012.)
6.  For those still struggling with this idea, look at this mind-blowing passage by the apostle Paul—the former *Christian-killer*: For you have heard of my previous way of life in Judaism, *how intensely I persecuted the church of God and tried to destroy it.* I was advancing in Judaism beyond many of my own age among my people and was extremely zealous for the traditions of my fathers. But when God, who set me apart from my mother's womb and called me by his grace, *was pleased to reveal his Son in me* so that I might preach him among the Gentiles … (Galatians 1:13-16, emphases mine). OK, let's stop there. Did you catch that? Paul, the former Christian-killer and legalist, claims that, *while* he was a Christian-killer and legalist, God was pleased to reveal His son *in* him (not to him). What the %*?#! I know, I know. How the heck did that passage get into your Bible just now?
7.  This is also the title of her book *Where There Is Love, There Is God: A Path to Closer Union with God and Greater Love for Others* (New York: Doubleday Religion, 2010), 7.
8.  I share this story the same way I heard Campolo share it during his interview. It can also be found in more detail in the book he co-authored with Shaine Claiborne called *Red Letter Revolution: What If Jesus Really Meant What He Said?* (Nashville, TN: Thomas Nelson, 2012), 53-54.
9.  I highly recommend everyone to read Wm. Paul Young's

book *The Shack* (Newbury Park, CA: Windblown Media, 2007). The quote is found on page 184.

## 5) THE CROSS: The Schizophrenic God

1.  I highly recommend the book edited by Brad Jersak and Michael Hardin called *Stricken by God?: Nonviolent Identification and the Victory of Christ* (Grand Rapids, MI: William B. Eerdmans, 2007). It is a collection of essays by some of the finest scholars today who are, thankfully, challenging and rejecting penal substitution and offering alternative atonement theories.
2.  I first heard it put this way by my friend, Raborn Johnson, on the *Beyond the Box* podcast episode called "Atonement, Part 1: Penal Substitution." (*Beyond the Box.* 18 Sept. 2009.) Raborn and his co-host, Steve Sensenig, have an awesome series where they discuss the strengths and weaknesses of some of the major atonement theories held throughout church history.
3.  See Isaiah 53:10.
4.  Author Steve Chalke describes penal substitution this way in his book *The Lost Message of Jesus* (Grand Rapids, MI: Zondervan, 2003), 182.
5.  I highly recommend Derek Flood's book *Healing the Gospel* (Eugene, OR: Wipf & Stock, 2012). Derek goes through just about every Scripture folks have learned to read in the context of penal substitution. He does a fine job showing how to read them restoratively.
6.  I'm extremely grateful for the insights concerning God's forgiveness in Brad Jersak's essay in *Stricken by God?* and Sharon Baker's book *Razing Hell* (Louisville, KY: Westminister John Knox Press, 2010), chapter 8.
7.  Check out Rene Girard's book *The Scapegoat* (Baltimore, MD: Johns Hopkins University Press, 1989) and Michael Hardin's *The Jesus Driven Life: Reconnecting Humanity With Jesus* (Lancaster, PA: JDL Press, 2010).

## 6) HELL: Too Hot to Handle

1.  Some of the best books I've read on the topic of hell are Brad Jersak's *Her Gates Will Never Be Shut: Hell, Hope, and the New Jerusalem* (Eugene, OR: Wipf & Stock, 2009); Julie Ferwerda's *Raising Hell: Christianity's Most Controversial Doctrine Put Under Fire* (Lander, WY: Vagabond Group, 2011); Sharon Baker's Razing Hell (Louisville, KY: Westminister John Knox Press, 2010); and Rob Bell's *Love Wins: A Book About Heaven, Hell, and the Fate of Every Person Who Ever Lived* (New York: HarperOne, 2011).

2.  I first started thinking along these lines in relation to hell when I read Gregory MacDonald's *The Evangelical Universalist* (Eugene, OR: Wipf & Stock, 2006). Gregory MacDonald is actually a pseudo name. The real name of the author is Robin Parry, who revealed his identity several years ago. Check out the book. It's good.

3.  It's such a powerful question. I started to really dwell on this thought when I heard Robin Parry's interview on the podcast *You're Included.* ("Hope for All Humanity." Online video clip. *You're Included.* Grace Communion International, 2013).

4.  I heard Rob Bell ask this question in a debate he did on the *Unbelievable?* podcast. ("Heaven & Hell." Online video clip. *Unbelievable?* Premier Christian Media, 2014.)

5.  In Jeremiah 7:30-31 it says the people of Judah did evil in the eyes of the Lord by sacrificing their children in a literal fire, which God said was something he *did not command nor did it enter his mind.* So why would God think this way back then when, nowadays, he supposedly has no problem burning the majority of his creation in a fire forever? Why the sudden change of heart?

6.  I put the word "evil" in quotes, because I personally don't believe people are inherently evil. I believe people have screwed up mindsets, which enable them to do stupid things. To me, people are just straight up awesome ... and loved. But if they only knew it.

7. This point stood out to me when I first read Julie Ferwerda's *Raising Hell* (Lander, WY: Vagabond Group, 2011), Kindle edition. In the book, she talks about the Jews ending up in an eternal hell with their torturer, Adolf Hitler.

8. Check out Kevin Miller's provocative, feature-length documentary *Hellbound?* (2012). It's a film which challenges the traditional view of hell and centers around the issue of whether God's justice is retributive or restorative. After watching it, you'll probably never see hell the same way again.

9. Should we be surprised? After all, it's found in Revelation 22:17.

## 7) SATAN: The Other Scapegoat

1. I first heard it put this way by James Brayshaw. One of his books goes by this title, which I highly recommend: *Satan, Christianity's Other God: Legend, Myth, Lore, or Lie* (Bloomington, IN: iUniverse, 2009).

2. Information on Satan's evolution is found in the documentary called *The History of the Devil* (Dir. Greg Moodie, 2007).

3. For the years I was more conservative theologically and serving at a Southern Baptist church (early 2000's), I didn't encounter any scary demonic activity. During this period, all I did was focus on getting people into the Bible and helping them to become moral. (Actually, more like legalistic, but I didn't know it at the time.) No focus on devils. No rebuking evils. No scary demonic manifestations in people's bodies. In fact, those weird and scary manifestations only started to happen once again when my theology became more "charismatic." And I say "once again" because, prior to my conservative days, I grew up in a Pentecostal church where those things occurred once in awhile.

4. You might be thinking, "Well, then can the same be said for belief in God as well?" I remember sharing this question with my friend, Bishop Carlton Pearson. I resonate with his

answer so much. Rather than paraphrase, let me share his own words: *As curious and spiritually oriented humans, we have inherited, enhanced, and created our particular gods. We all believe something, but actually know little with full resolution. We choose what to believe and not believe, usually based on the hand-me-down and often cherished opinions of others. Knowledge is innate and intrinsic only to spirit....God is what we remember (know) in the deepest recesses of our souls. God is not religion or religious, except the imaginary one we have made up or manufactured and must maintain and even defend.* Bishop Carlton Pearson sent this to me as we exchanged private messages online. He is a brilliant thinker who has an amazing book called *God Is Not a Christian, Nor a Jew, Muslim, Hindu...: God Dwells with Us, in Us, Around Us, as Us* (New York, NY: Atria Books, 2010). He's been an inspiration to me and has definitely paved the way for many people to question their long-held religious beliefs.

5.  How do we make sense of the time when Jesus turns to Peter and says, "Get behind me, Satan!" (Matthew 16:23)? How do we make sense of the time when Jesus referred to one of his disciples as a "devil" (John 6:70)? Could "Satan" or "devil" in the Bible sometimes be referring to a *human* adversary?

6.  There are a number of good books you could read on this subject. There's Walter Wink's *The Powers That Be: Theology for a New Millennium* (New York: Galilee, 1998), reprint edition; *Unmasking the Powers: The Invisible Forces that Determine Human Existence* (Philadelphia: Fortress Press, 1986); Rene Girard's *I See Satan Fall Like Lightning* (Maryknoll, NY: Orbis, 2006 reprint); and *Understanding Spiritual Warfare: Four Views* (Grand Rapids, MI: Baker Academic, 2012) edited by James K. Beilby and Paul Rhodes Eddy.

## 8) INTERFAITH: Building Bridges

1.  Brian McLaren has an awesome book on the topic of "interfaith" and "the other" called *Why Did Jesus, Moses, the Buddha, and Mohammed Cross the Road?: Christian Identity in a Multi-Faith World* (New York: Jericho Books, 2012).
2.  It's true. Although the Qur'an contains violent stories, surprisingly, the Bible is filled with even more violence. And just as not every Muslim is the same, not every Christian is the same either. In fact, Christian and Muslim fundamentalists tend to look alike when it comes to exclusivity, intolerance, and violence.
3.  This is not to say that I don't know of any Christians exemplifying peace. My point is that others have found peace, who are part of other traditions. I've even heard Christians judge Buddhists as having "false peace." Maybe. But many Buddhists sure seem peaceful and compassionate to me even though it may be "false." Maybe we should stop judging people's hearts.
4.  I encourage people to not use friendship as a means to an end (i.e., conversion), but to look at friendship as an end. Cherish people for being just that—people. People are awesome.
5.  I'm sure there are unkind people in every religion. No exceptions. I'm simply sharing my own experience growing up as a Christian.
6.  *The Human Experience* (Dir. Charles Kinnane. Grassroots Films, 2008.) I highly recommend for people to watch it.
7.  Matthew 25:40 (NIV) says, "The King will reply, 'Truly I tell you, whatever you did for one of the least of these brothers and sisters of mine, you did for me.'"
8.  Acts 17:26-27 (NIV) says, "From one man he made all the nations, that they should inhabit the whole earth; and he marked out their appointed times in history and the boundaries of their lands. God did this so that they would seek him and perhaps reach out for him and find him, though he is not far from any of us."

## 9) CHURCH: A Beautiful Mess

1. For one of the best books on the pagan origins of institutional church practices, check out Frank Viola and George Barna's controversial (and eye-opening) book *Pagan Christianity?: Exploring the Roots of Our Church Practices* (BarnaBooks; Revised edition, 2008).
2. Some people enjoy attending large weekly church services. Others don't. To each his (or her) own. We all desire and need different things at different times.
3. I never called myself "pastor" while I lived in the Philippines. Nor did I ask anyone to call me by that title (although some people considered me their pastor). I'm not against titles, per se, but I refrain from using them at times because they can somewhat create a distance between people. I wanted people to feel comfortable and to "be real" around me.
4. I highly recommend reading Wayne Jacobsen and Dave Coleman's book *So You Don't Want to Go to Church Anymore: An Unexpected Journey* (Newbury Park, CA: Windblown Media, 2006). It seriously "messed me up" in a good way.
5. Sure, a lot of the people who used to attend our Sunday service in the beginning no longer hung out with us. But for me, it was OK. I was looking for authentic friendships, not church-service or ministry-based ones.
6. There's nothing wrong with praying or quoting Bible verses, but in my experience, it's not always the best thing to do in every situation like this. We need to shake-off religiosity and go with the flow.

## 10) LETTING GO (Conclusion)

1. This story can be found at Remy Tongol's website. ("Struggling with a Life Jacket." Remytongol.com.)

# ACKNOWLEDGMENTS

—A SHOUT-OUT TO ALL MY PEEPS—

**My parents (Ismael and Aurea)** for bringing me into this world and loving me unconditionally

**My sisters (Karen and Melorie)** - who would've thought your crazy little brother—who used to jump off rooftops and pretend to be Bruce Lee as a kid—would write a book one day?

**My close friends in the USofA and Philippines** who showed me what it means to "be the church." My understanding of authentic community has never been the same

**Alicia Mendez** for being an amazing and patient editor

**Brendon James** for for making this book look fantastic. You've got some mad designing skillz, homie.

**The critics** who help spread this message without even realizing it

**The local Starbucks** for being my second "office" where this book was written

**All the b-boys and b-girls** on YouTube who entertained me whenever I needed to take a break from writing

**Those who reviewed the manuscript and gave helpful feedback.** These awesome peeps are: Brad Jersak, Kevin Miller, Carlton Pearson, Michael Hardin, Derek Flood, Sharon Baker, and Raborn Johnson. Their input has made this book much better

**Remy** ... for loving me the way you do

# ABOUT THE AUTHOR

**Joshua Tongol** is a graduate of Biola University and Talbot School of Theology. He is a popular speaker who travels the world sharing the message of God's love. He lives in California with his fun and amazing wife, Remy.

If you want to stay connected with Josh, you can visit the following:

**WEBSITE**
joshuatongol.com

**YOUTUBE**
youtube.com/user/joshuat77

**FACEBOOK**
facebook.com/joshuatongolpage

**TWITTER**
twitter.com/joshuatongol

CPSIA information can be obtained at www.ICGtesting.com
Printed in the USA
BVOW05s0314221014

371751BV00004B/308/P